American Bards & The London Reviewer: A Satire

by Pietros Maneos

Pietros Maneos

American Bards & The London Reviewer: A Satire
1st Edition

About the Author:
Pietros Maneos, a graduate of The University of Miami, is the author of the poetry collections, *The Soul of a Young Man* and *Poems of Blood and Passion* as well as the internationally acclaimed novella, *The Italian Pleasures of Gabriele Paterkallos*. For more information, visit www.pietrosmaneos.com.

ISBN 978-0-9852281-4-9
© 2014 – Aesthete Press / Pietros Maneos
This first edition is published by Aesthete Press.
Cover painting: "To Kalon" by Tomasz Rut (oil on Canvas, 2011, private collection). Artwork copyright © Tomasz Rut.
Cover design by novelist/designer Roman Payne (www.romanpayne.com).

For more information, visit www.aesthetepress.com.

To 'The Beautiful' and the dwindling aristocracy of its apostles.

'To make verse which would scan and rhyme as well, to search out and harmonise the measure of every syllable and unite it to the swift, flitting, swallow-like motion of rhyme, to penetrate their poetry with a double music, - this was the ambition of the *Pleiad*. They are insatiable of music, they cannot have enough of it; they desire a music of greater compass perhaps than words can possibly yield, to drain out the last drops of sweetness which a certain note or accent contains.' – Walter Pater

'When Fadayev declared in Wroclaw that, if hyenas used a pen or a typewriter they would write like T.S. Eliot or the novelist Sartre, I think that was an insult to the animal kingdom. I do not believe that creatures endowed with intelligence and the power of expression would make such an obscene religion out of the annihilation and repugnant vice, as those two so-called 'masters' of Western culture have done.' – Pablo Neruda

'For just a little while longer, we hold the heights, the realm of the aesthetic.' – Harold Bloom

'My entire soul is a cry, and all my work is a commentary on that cry.' – Nikos Kazantzakis

Author's Introduction

This work is rooted in my feeling of alienation from the prevailing poetic and artistic traditions of the 20th and the 21st centuries. It seems that many artists from these eras are concerned with the rebellion from form, the defense of form, innovation for innovation's sake, multiculturalism, bohemianism, genderism, and so on and so forth, but that very few are interested in aesthetic creation. Art that serves the sublime idea of beauty is devalued as traditional, unoriginal, and unimportant. The noble Greek concept of *To Kalon* – 'The Beautiful' – has been relegated to an ancient time, not a principle praised in modern culture.

Furthermore, I believe that this manuscript, meticulously crafted over twelve years, transcends the label of a poem and ascends into the realm of a 'cultural document.' In my estimation, this holds true even if one comes to disagree with the sentiments expressed herein, for I have managed to marry literature with literary criticism and scholarship with artistry. It will be left to posterity, of course, to determine whether I have done this successfully or not, but to the best of my knowledge the amalgamation of such disparate elements into one manuscript is completely novel.

Specifically, I satirize T.S. Eliot (high-culture), Charles Bukowski (low-culture), Allen Ginsberg (counter-culture) and Frank O'Hara (avant-garde culture). Each poet was carefully chosen, not only for their individual poetry, but also for what each writer has come to symbolize within the culture at large. T.S. Eliot, the most prominent poet of the Modernist movement, reacted against many of the Romantic and Aesthetic writers with whom I relate. Eliot's depressive, Anglophilic, Anglican leanings could not be further from my own sentiments, and his dissonant, minimalist style could not be further from my own operatic, evocative writing style. Eliot looks to London, and to England in general, for poetic sustenance, while I possess a bit of Delacroix's Romantic Orientalism, a Mediterranean wanderlust.

Where Eliot writes poetry when he is out of health, I write from joy, from passion, in between moments of ecstasy, tragedy and Dionysian dances. My Dionysus however is not the Dionysus of Woodstock, awash in urine and feces, stinking of marijuana, overcome by LSD, but rather the true God, as interpreted by Euripides, Nonnus, Antony, Michelangelo, Nietzsche, and Kazantzakis, not by Jack Kerouac, William Burroughs, or Allen Ginsberg. My Dionysus is perfumed with fragrant incense, garlanded in exotic flowers, with the blood of grapes, the oil of olives, and the nectar of honey dripping down his flesh; he is grasping his thyrsus in one hand and his kylix in the other, dancing to the most exquisitely beautiful music alongside his panthers, leopards, and maenads; this is not the God distorted by the hippies of the 1960s and transformed into a plebeian caricature, a shabby farce, for my Dionysus is the beautiful God, the savage God, still alive, dancing to the timbrel, in all of his immense and immortal glory.

Charles Bukowski, the master of The Vulgar, the fêted nihilist, has become something of a cult phenomenon in modern culture. It seems that those who reject Eliot's style of poetry as priggish, esoteric, and frigid retreat into this type of poetry. It has become a haven for Hipsters, a type of sustenance, an ambrosia, for their sensibility. Some of Bukowski's critics find fault in his morals, or lack thereof, but this is not my objection, as I am closer to Walter Pater in my protestations than to Girolamo Savaronola, Marcus Tullius Cicero, or Cyril of Alexandria; it is not Bukowski's louche living that I find fault with, as much of my own poetry is decadent, but rather Bukowski's sense of aesthetics; his is a poetry devoid of any poetry.

Another tenet of Bukowski's aesthetic, or more accurately, anti-aesthetic, is a strong strain of nihilism. Now, like many other nihilists, I am sure that Bukowski and his modern lackeys would take umbrage at this label, as they prefer to title themselves 'Realists,' for they are merely portraying the world as it truly is: a place that is horrible, despicable, and filled with despair; they sneeringly dismiss any who object to their gloomy perspective as a callow naïf outfitted in rose-tinted glasses. But I would like to remind both Bukowski, and his legions of living descendants, that every Winter is followed by Spring, that abject despair has its counterpoint in effusive joy, and that for every lost love, there is renewed love.

Allen Ginsberg, although different from Bukowski in many ways, is similar in his anti-aesthetic pose. The form and style of the Ginsberg section within this satire differs from the other three sections. In the Ginsberg section, I have chosen just one single poem to satirize, his *America*, instead of a collection of fragments. Also, unlike the other three sections where I counter as myself, in this section I have morphed into a Beat/Dirty Realist/Hipster poet in both content and style for maximum comic and ironic effect; it is deliberately a bad poem. I have mirrored my nemesis and his modern acolytes in order to illuminate the absurdity of their verse.

The satire finishes with Frank O'Hara, the de facto poetic representative of The New York School/Abstract Expressionism, a movement that also adheres to the anti-aesthetic belief; the idea of striving for aesthetic beauty is considered passé to both O'Hara and his comrades, for they are more concerned with innovation than with beauty. O'Hara's constant allusions to these artists afford me a perfect opportunity to spar with their brand of aesthetics. In my view, O'Hara also partakes in the excesses of surrealism, which reduces much of his verse to randomly strewn together gibberish, as if words were placed into a satchel, shaken vigorously, and then thrown upon the page; this tendency is in stark contrast to the aesthetic surrealism one finds in the poetry of Andre Breton, specifically his lovely poem *Free Union*, one of the great triumphs of 20th century poetry. Additionally, O'Hara finds comfort in the New York milieu whereas I long for the environs of the Mediterranean.

I've discovered that when one criticizes Eliot and his ilk, one is often summarily dismissed as just another anti-form Beat proponent who doesn't have the intellectual depth, the emotional sensitivity, or the nuanced soul, to appreciate and admire Eliot's poetry. Now, when one dares to criticize Ginsberg, Bukowski, and other Beat writers for their lack of verbal beauty, their lack of poetic craft, one is immediately tagged as a neo-formalist, just another stuffed shirt academic, part of the cabal of tenured university professors, conservative readers, and private school English departments allied against the Beats, who don't comprehend the zeitgeist of the era. My response is – I understand you – and I reject you thoroughly and completely.

This 'poem' is not simply a rejection of ascendant cultural mores, but rather a *cri de coeur* for Romantic ideals. If this satire was merely a tirade, 'The Great No,' it would be nothing more than the work of a shrill curmudgeon, a ranting contrarian, and my intent is certainly not to wallow in iconoclasm. The question then becomes, what does a resurrection of Romanticism mean? Well, for one, a rise of poetry that is once again musical. Poetry, invented by the ancient Greeks, was originally sung to the lyre, where we derive the word 'lyric.' Much of this satire was written to the sonorous sounds of the Cretan lyra. So, when I compose something like 'An osprey flew over the sea-shimmering sea-spray/Careening past where the dreamy nymphs play,[1]' or 'that ascends like a cresting crescendo of light[2]' the musicality is directly drawn from the lyra. The intense internal rhyming that one will find within a single line is anathema to much of modern poetry, which often flaunts its absence of rhyme.

By writing and editing to the lyra and sometimes the bouzouki, both instruments blessed by Orpheus himself, my poetry effortlessly attains the Paterian 'double music.' One would have to return to Swinburne's majestic lines like, 'came flushed from the full-flushed wave[3]' and 'Fearful fitful wings of the doves departing,[4]' to find a comparison to the ravishing musicality of a single poetic line. What of metaphors soaring to the heights of Parnassus? What of similes simmering and seething with light? What of assonance, consonance and alliteration? Besides being musically inclined, the Romantic also possesses an idealistic world-view, which contrasts directly with the cynical, nihilistic writing of those whom I have chosen to satirize; the modern artist has fallen deeply in love with irony, wit, and sarcasm whereas I worship beauty, passion, and emotion. Maybe I am alone in my belief that pessimism is not tantamount to wisdom.

The Romantic transforms *The Wasteland* into *The Land of Milk and Honey*, *Waiting for Godot* becomes *Godot and Juliet*, and J. Alfred Prufrock miraculously (and thankfully) transmogrifies into Count Almasy. Nature, passion, love, emotion, experience, hero-worship, dreams, and wanderlust are embraced by the Romantic, among other things. The Romantic also shuns the idea of an 'impersonal poetry' as promulgated by T.S. Eliot, for the Romantic creates a very personal poetry; the Romantic does not flee from emotion, but rather works from emotion, in all of its multifarious manifestations, for poetry is a triumph of the individual spirit, the very blood of the soul.

The format of this satire is unique in that I have excerpted the actual verses of the writers mentioned in order to counter their work directly. In most cases, I follow the basic structure of my adversary in the ensuing stanza so as to illuminate the vast difference in both theme and style. This innovative form, this 'literary argument,' developed organically, the result of passion, not of reason. For example, when I was reading T.S. Eliot in the Villa Borghese, flanked by the gorgeous, glorious statues of Byron and Pushkin, and came across, 'No! I am not Prince Hamlet, nor was meant to be;[5]' I had to restrain myself from shouting aloud, 'Yes! I am Prince Hamlet and was meant to be;[6]'

It is my sincere hope that this satire not only inspires the individual reader, but also other artists working in diverse mediums; in my incessant dreams, my mad visions, I imagine that it sparks a neo-Romantic, neo-Aesthetic movement as did Walter Pater's famous conclusion in *Studies in the History of the Renaissance*. Time will tell, I suppose. Maybe I will be the only one marching to The Hot Gates to face The Barbarians. So be it.

Maybe The Barbarians are too numerous, too powerful, too entrenched to defeat, but I still will be true to my sense of aesthetics, and stand firmly at Thermopylae, fighting in the shade, throwing my quixotic spear, even if 'in the end the Medes will go through.⁷'

I

Satire, be now your song, oh immortal Calliope.
Begin to sing of a new era:
A Renaissance of Beauty in modernity,
where irony and cynicism
are replaced by a novel expression
of Romantic Aestheticism.

Please, oh glowing Calliope,
Bestow your eternal graces upon my mortal quill,
grace my fine lines in divine linens,
and fill my trilling Soul with your indomitable Will.

So let us now return to the glistening glens of Arcadia,
garlanded in the Roses of Pieria
while serving the burning lyra of Mytilene.
Given to the dreams
and the passions
of the impassioned Olympians.

II

Eliot writes:
'No! I am not Prince Hamlet, nor was meant to be;   8
Am an attendant lord, one that will do
To swell a progress, start a scene or two,
Advise the prince;'

Maneos counters:
'Yes! I am Prince Hamlet and was meant to be;
Am not an attendant lord, but the King with the swaggering sword –
The one who fords novel rivers,
And the one who checks the barbarian hordes.'

Eliot quotes:
'I saw with my own eyes the Sibyl at Cumae,   9
suspended in a cage, and when the boys
asked her, "Sibyl, what do you want?," she
replied, "I want to die."

Maneos counters:
'I saw with my own eyes Romeo in Hades,
Suspended within a cavernous cage, decrepit and grossly aged.
And when I asked him, 'Romeo, what do you want?'
He replied with a single word, 'Juliet.''

Eliot writes:
'Here I am, an old man in a dry month   10
Being read to by a boy, waiting for rain.
I was neither at the hot gates
Nor fought in the warm rain.'

Maneos counters:
'Here I am, a young man in a warm month
Reading to myself, waiting for the morning storm.
Not only was I at The Hot Gates,
But I eagerly await my Cyprian Fate.'

Eliot writes:
'I have lost my passion: why should I need to keep it   11
Since what is kept must be adulterated?
I have lost my sight, smell, hearing, taste and touch:
How should I use them for your closer contact?'

Maneos counters:
'I am the very definition of Passion!
For the burning blood of Sappho flows through my poetry.
I have not lost my sight, smell, hearing, taste or touch:
In fact, I've just finished tasting and touching a Finnish miss.'

Eliot writes:
'The only wisdom we can hope to acquire   12
Is the wisdom of humility: humility is endless.

The houses are all gone under the sea.

The dancers are all gone under the hill.'

Maneos counters:

'The only wisdom we can hope to acquire
Is the wisdom of Pride – Pride is Eternal:

Achilles: 'Not if his gifts outnumbered the sea-sands   13
or all of the dust-grains in the world could Agamemnon
ever appease me not till he pays me back full measure,
pain for pain, dishonor for dishonor.'

Odysseus: 'Eurymachos, if you gave me all your father's   14
possessions, all that you have now, and what you could
add from elsewhere, even so, I would not stay my hands
from the slaughter, until I had taken revenge for all the
suitors' transgression.'

Leonidas: 'Molon Labe!'   15

Dianeces: 'All to the good, my friend from Trachis.   16
If the Persians hide the sun, the battle will be in the
shade rather than sunlight.'

Aeschylus: 'Of his noble prowess the grove of Marathon   17
can speak, or the long-haired Persian who knows it well.'

Gaius Mucius: 'I am Gaius Mucius, a citizen of Rome.   18
I came here as an enemy to kill my enemy,
and I am as ready to die as I am to kill.'

Dania: 'And if the Turks fix our heads to their battlements   19
those remains will be a lesson how brave men are prepared
to die for liberty and their beliefs.'

Metaxas: 'OXI!'   20

Seal Team Six: 'Geronimo EKIA'   21

The houses are not gone under the sea.

The dancers still dance in the Theban hills! Ehoi! Ehoi!'

Eliot writes:

'We are the hollow men   22
We are the stuffed men
Leaning together
Headpiece filled with straw. Alas!
Our dried voices, when
We whisper together
Are quiet and meaningless
As wind in dry grass
Or rats' feet over broken glass
In our dry cellar'

Maneos counters:
'We are the Heroic Men
We are the Brave Men
Fighting together,
Breast-plates dripping with blood. Ehoi!
Our collective battle-cry,
when screamed in unison,
rattles Persia's Sons.
Go tell them, stranger passing by,
That here, a Pride of stubborn Lions lie.'

Eliot writes:
'Remember us – if at all – not as lost   23
Violent souls, but only
As the hollow men
The stuffed men.'

Maneos counters:
'Remember us – if at all – not as losing rebels
but as defiant heroes.
The ones who dared to spit into the wintry wind –
dared to defy the deified scarecrows.'

Eliot writes:
'I am no prophet – and here's no great matter;   24
I have seen the moment of my greatness flicker,
And I have seen the eternal Footman hold my coat, and snicker,
And in short, I was afraid.'

Maneos counters:
'I am an ancient augur – and here's a great matter;
War with an Arabian-Asian alliance draws closer,
And yet the question remains – how sharp is our saber?
Will we, the land of the free, have the capacity to counter?'

Eliot writes:
'Nothing here   25
But the warm
Dry airless sweet scent
Of the alleys of death
Of the corridors of death'

Maneos counters:
'Nothing here
But the warm
Sweet scent
Of the valleys soaked with Life
Of the shores drenched with Passion'

Eliot writes:
'Since our concern was speech, and speech impelled us   26
To purify the dialect of the tribe
And urge the mind to aftersight and foresight,'

Maneos counters:
'Since our concern was Passion, and Passion compelled us
To purify the Soul of the tribe
And urge the body to the heights of sensual delights.'

Eliot writes:
'Defunctive music under sea   27
    Passed seaward with the passing bell
Slowly: the God Hercules
    Had left him, that had loved him well.'

Maneos counters:
'Melodious music raining from the sea
Passed seaward with the passing seagulls –
Passionately: the God Hercules, full beautiful,

And full of Love returned faithfully
with the immortal belt of Hippolyte.'

Eliot writes:
"If the lady and gentleman
wish to take their tea in the garden, if the lady and gentleman wish
to take their tea in the garden. . ." I decided that if the shaking of
her breasts could be stopped, some of the fragments of the afternoon
might be collected, and I concentrated my attention with careful
subtlety to this end.'

Maneos counters:
"If the lady and the gentleman
wish to take their wine in the atrium, if the lady and the gentleman
wish to take their wine in the atrium. . .' I decided that if the shaking
of her breasts could be prolonged, some of the moments of this wine-
kissed afternoon might be turned into a wild song, a song of blood and
passion, and so I concentrated my attention with searing intensity to
this end.'

Eliot writes:
'And indeed there will be time
To wonder, "Do I dare?" and, "Do I dare?"
Time to turn back and descend the stair,
With a bald spot in the middle of my hair –'

Maneos counters:
'Seize The Day! (what a wonderful cliché)
For today may be the day
When you are chosen to descend into Hades,
To forever sleep with the Furies.'

Eliot writes:
'But at my back in a cold blast I hear
The rattle of the bones, and chuckle spread from ear to ear.'

Maneos counters:
'But at my back I always seem to hear
Eliot's rats teaching the learned how to sneer.'

28

29

30

Eliot writes:
'And the jew squats on the window sill, the owner,   31
Spawned in some estaminet of Antwerp,
Blistered in Brussels, patched and peeled in London.'

Maneos counters:
'My friend, Uri, the Israeli
Often composes poesy celebrating the Sicarii,
The Martyrs of Masada,
Who preferred death to slavery,
And whose souls live on heroically,
Dancing on the waves of The Dead Sea!'

Eliot writes:
'Philosophy through a paper straw!'   32

Maneos counters:
'Poetry sung to the lyre!'

III

Eliot writes:
'April is the cruellest month, breeding   33
Lilacs out of the dead land, mixing
Memory and desire, stirring
Dull roots with spring rain.
Winter kept us warm, covering
Earth in forgetful snow, feeding
A little life with dried tubers.'

Maneos counters:
'April is the loveliest month of the year,
Sprouting lilacs out of the flowering hillocks,
Bursting with springing loves, and budding desires,
And cajoling flower-beds with its raining-tears.
Spring gives us Hope, showering
The Earth with gifts of flowers, prisms of color, visions of doves
Nourishing our Souls with a little bit of celestial Love.'

Eliot writes:

' Since golden October declined into sombre November   34
And the apples were gathered and stored, and the land became
    brown sharp points of death in a waste of water and mud,'

Maneos counters:
'Since golden October descended into silken November
When the red apples were gathered with sea-battered sea-shells,
The land became a gorgeous garden:
Poignant points of light fell
into my hidden glen –
my private haven brimming with carnations, impatiens,
and geraniums.'

Eliot writes:
'The winter evening settles down   35
With the smell of steaks in passageways.
Six o'clock.'

Maneos counters:
'The spring evening settles down
With the ambrosial aromas of cassia and cassidony all around.
Seven o'clock.'

Eliot writes:
'The morning comes to consciousness   36
Of faint stale smells of beer
From the sawdust trampled street
With its muddy feet
that pass
To early coffee stands-'

Maneos counters:
'The morning blooms like a field filled with singing jasmine.
The bouquet of wine and the scent of rose
Interrupt my soothing repose
With my newfound friend.'

Eliot writes:
'This charm of vacant lots!   37
The helpless fields that lie

Sinister, sterile and blind'

Maneos counters:
'This charm of sylvan glens!
The laughter of friends
that ascends like a cresting crescendo of light
Buoyant, ebullient and jubilant!'

Eliot writes:
'The river sweats   38
Oil and tar'

Maneos counters:
'The wind-shivering river sweats
blood, jasmine and honeysuckle.'

Eliot writes:
'I think we are in rats' alley   39
Where the dead men lost their bones.'

Maneos counters:
'I think butterflies fly through our souls –
Psyche told me so in a dream.'

Eliot writes:
'The rats are underneath the piles.   40
The jew is underneath the lot.
Money in furs. The boatman smiles,'

Maneos counters:
'Baby butterflies flutter past the buttercups
Like angels flying through heaven –
Savoring their first taste of pollen
in my heavenly garden.'

Eliot writes:
'A rat crept softly through the vegetation   41
Dragging its slimy belly on the bank
While I was fishing in the dull canal'

Maneos counters:
'An osprey flew over the sea-shimmering sea-spray
Careening past where the dreamy nymphs play,
While I was diving into the lively bay.'

Eliot writes:
'This is the dead land   42
This is cactus land
Here the stone images
Are raised, here they receive
The supplication of a dead man's hand
Under the twinkle of a fading star.'

Maneos counters:
'This is the thriving land
For bands of fragrant flowers span the entire horizon,
like strands of spiraling night-fire coloring a forbidden garden.
Here they receive the supplication of Byron's poetic hand
Under the twinkling twilight of a wondrous constellation.'

Eliot writes:
'In a brown field stood a tree   43
And the tree was crookt and dry.
In a black sky, from a green cloud
Natural forces shriek'd aloud,
Screamed, rattled, muttered endlessly.'

Maneos counters:
'In a flourishing field stood a tremendous tree.
And the tree was as magisterial as a Roman magistrate
As magical as gypsy poetry sung melodiously in the Trastevere,
And as divine as the very vines entwining the brow of Hermes.

Under a violet sky, from a thunderous cloud
Nature unfurled her majestic power, aloud.
For lightning tore through the furious sky like a torrid beam of light.'

Eliot writes:
'no wind, but pentecostal fire   44
In the dark time of the year. Between melting and freezing

The soul's sap quivers. There is no earth smell
Or smell of living thing. This is the spring time
But not in time's covenant. Now the hedgerow
Is blanched for an hour with transitory blossom
Of snow, a bloom more sudden
Than that of summer, neither budding nor fading,
Not in the scheme of generation.
Where is the summer, the unimaginable
Zero summer?'

Maneos counters:
'Here are the songs of Spring!
Ay, here they are!
Sent forth from the whispering wind
to win the Souls of Men worshipping
the doctrine of Nothing.

Ay, here they are!
Springing from a single shining star,
And descending into singing springs –
Flowing freely like poetry from a Hindi Sitar.

Ay, here they are!
Bringing the soothing music of the Cosmos
through the winnowing wings of rosy-fingered Eos
into the comely coast of Lesbos –
Where it soothes the bruised soul of Orpheus.'

Eliot writes:
'A heap of broken images, where the sun beats,   45
And the dead tree gives no shelter, the cricket no relief,
And the dry stone no sound of water. Only
There is shadow under this red rock,
(Come in under the shadow of this red rock),
And I will show you something different from either
Your shadow at morning striding behind you
Or your shadow at evening rising to meet you
I will show you fear in a handful of dust.'

Maneos counters:

'A collage of immaculate images, where the sun beats
down upon them, like a cataclysm of glimmering gems.
The blossoming tree provides shade,
The song-thrush sings songs flushed with lush paeans,
And the water gently flows into the gentle glade.
(Come in under the shadow of this flower-kissed mountain),
And take a sip from this timeless fountain,
Before I show you something different from
Your present ideology or your Modern philosophy,
I will show you the Almighty living in this very greenery!'

Eliot writes:
'Every street-lamp that I pass   46
Beats like a fatalistic drum,
And through the spaces of the dark
Midnight shakes the memory
As a madman shakes a dead geranium.'

Maneos counters:
'Every street-lamp that I pass
Blazes like a thousand suns emblazoned
with the raging light of moonlit diamonds.
And through the silent spaces stitched into the night
the moonlight stirs the Passions
as a madman dancing in a field of geraniums.'

Eliot writes:
'Geraniums, geraniums   47
On a third-floor window sill.
Their perfume comes
With the smell of heat
From the asphalt street.
Geraniums geraniums
Withered and dry
Long laid by
In the sweepings of the memory.'

Maneos counters:
'Geraniums! Geraniums!
Blooming in my Babylonian garden.

Their perfume mingles with the aroma
of Persian-gardenia,
eliciting exquisite ecstasy,
among my gathered company.

Geraniums! Geraniums!
Luxurious and Luscious
And as glorious
as the glinting sun
when it fervently runs
into the horizon.'

Eliot writes:
'Daffodils
Long yellow sunlight fills
The cool secluded room
Swept and set in order –
Smelling of earth and rain.
And again
The insistent sweet perfume
And the impressions it preserves
Irritate the imagination
Or the nerves.'

Maneos counters:
'Daffodils and Jonquils grace my window sill.
Graceful, supernal sunlight fills
my sunlit room;
suffusing the library
with the eloquence
of supernatural beauty.

The persistent sweet-smelling perfume
Permeates the Palladian estate:
Delighting both the Senses
and the Soul.
Like soft kisses sent from the sensual Moon.'

Eliot writes:
'The moon has lost her memory.

A washed-out smallpox cracks her face,
Her hand twists a paper rose,
That smells of dust and old Cologne,'

Maneos counters:
'The magnificent moon, that crescent of light,
That sickle of blissful mystery,
Whose alabaster eyes are burnished with ivory,
burned with ichor and bursting with lapis lazuli.

The perennial moon! The mercurial moon! The imperial moon!
Whose long fingers caress a carnal rose
Whose primal songs descend into deserted deserts,
and whose body is as proudly curved as a bent sword
that has tasted the flesh of Immortality.'

Eliot writes:
'Dead water and dead sand   50
Contending for the upper hand.
The parched eviscerate soil
Gapes at the vanity of toil,
Laughs without mirth.
This is the death of earth.'

Maneos counters:
'Flowing water and glowing sand
Comprise this convivial land.
These fecund, fertile hills
Oppose the grit-filled mills.
This is the rebirth
Of the neglected Earth.'

IV

Eliot writes:
'On every sultry afternoon   51
Verandah customs have the call
White flannel ceremonial
With cakes and tea
And guesses at eternal truths'

Maneos counters:
'On every Sunday afternoon
Asiatic customs are the thing:
Rembetic tunes blare from the back-room
As we sing of ancient Grecian kings.'

Eliot writes:
'The showers beat   52
On broken blinds and chimney-pots,
And at the corner of the street
A lonely cab-horse steams and stamps.
And then the lighting of the lamps.'

Maneos counters:
'The feet beat
Upon the sturdy tables and sleek plates,
And in the corner of the Taverna
A lonely man demands the attention
Of the chanting gypsy band.
And then the shrill sound of the baglama:
Ah o baglamas!'

Eliot writes:
'I can sometimes hear   53
Beside a public bar in Lower Thames Street,
The pleasant whining of mandoline
And a clatter and a chatter from within
Where fishermen lounge at noon;'

Maneos counters:
'I can sometimes hear the cheers
From a cheerful taverna in smoldering Smyrna.
The winsome whining of the fine santouri,
The proclamations of the jeering women,
And the exclamations of the leering men,
Remind me of my timeless love for dancing in lines.
Opa!'

Eliot writes:
'Shall I say, I have gone at dusk through narrow streets   54
And watched the smoke that rises from the pipes
Of lonely men in shirt-sleeves, leaning out of windows? . . .

I should have been a pair of ragged claws
Scuttling across the floors of silent seas.'

Maneos counters:
'Shall I say, I have gone at dawn through the venues near the
Acropolis
And watched wily Katsimbalis make a fool of the cruel British,
While dancing like a whirling dervish? . . .
Cock-a-doodle-doo!

I should have been a sashaying satyr,
Touring the wooded Peloponnese in a woven sash hunting for singing
woodland nymphs.'

Eliot writes:
'we stopped in the colonnade,   55
And went on in sunlight, into the Hofgarten,
And drank coffee, and talked for an hour.
Bin gar keine Russin, stamm' aus Litauen, echt deutsch.'

Maneos counters:
'Under the Grecian moonbeams, we gazed at the Erechtheum,
Before praising the Parthenon.
We then retired to Gazi to sing to the kingly lyre:
'Εγώ Γραικός γεννήθηκα, Γραικός θε να πεθάνω"   56

Eliot writes:
'Shall I part my hair behind? Do I dare to eat a peach?'   57

Maneos counters:
'Shall I let my hair grow out like a doughty Spartan before
I dart into battle to tear apart the smarting Moors?'

Eliot writes:
'We hibernate among the bricks   58

And live across the window panes
With marmalade and tea at six'

Maneos counters:
'We dance the Hasapiko with a crazed butcher
And live within nature like an Arcadian hunter
With tsipouro and ouzo at four.'

Eliot writes:
'One thinks of all the hands   59
That are raising dingy shades
In a thousand furnished rooms.'

Maneos counters:
'One thinks of the fearless Spartan hands
That devised a bold plan
To face the faceless foreign bands.'

Eliot writes:
'Let me also wear   60
Such deliberate disguises
Rat's coat, crowskin, crossed staves'

Maneos counters:
'Let me also wear
Such ancient disguises
Himation, chiton, and greaves'

Eliot writes:
'The wind   61
Crosses the brown land, unheard. The nymphs are departed.'

Maneos counters:
'The wind
Slices through the window like a battalion of javelins.
The numinous nymphs are dancing to the singing of Arion.'

Eliot writes:
'By the water of Leman I sat down and wept. . .'   62

Maneos counters:
'By the water of Hebrus I sat down and wept:
Eurydice!'

Eliot writes:
'Wipe your hand across your mouth, and laugh;   63
The worlds revolve like ancient women
Gathering fuel in vacant lots.'

Maneos counters:
'Wipe the blood from your mouth, and Roar!
For the Iranian army circles like a violent vulture –
Impatiently waiting to end our ancient culture.'

Eliot writes:
'Unreal City   64
Under the brown fog of a winter noon
Mr. Eugenides, the Smyrna merchant
Unshaven, with a pocket full of currants
C.i.f London: documents at sight,
Asked me in demotic French
To luncheon at the Cannon Street Hotel
Followed by a weekend at the Metropole.'

Maneos counters:
'Burning city
Crawling in the snarling smoke of a torched polis,
while inhaling the scent of burnt flesh,
Mr. Kazantzakis, the Nietzschean Artist,
Vows vengeance against the tyrants of Turkey:
The sons of Mongols,
The cousins of Huns,
For one day Smyrna will be Free!'

Eliot writes:
'White bodies naked on the low damp ground   65
And bones cast in a little low dry garret,
Rattled by the rat's foot only, year to year.
But at my back from time to time I hear
The sound of horns and motors, which shall bring

Sweeney to Mrs. Porter in the spring.'

Maneos counters:
'Sun-lavished bodies languishing naked in Mytilene –
The nymphs and naiads swimming in a swaying stream
inspired by the fierce fire of Lesbian lyres.
And at my back, from time to time, I hear tender murmurs –
Pleadings, pantings, and sufferings wet with amorous desires
Which shall surely bring singing Aphrodite, the Paphian queen,
into these light-kissed waters.'

Eliot writes:
'There I saw one I knew, and stopped him, crying: 'Stetson!   66
'You who were with me in the ships at Mylae!
'That corpse you planted last year in your garden,
'Has it begun to sprout? Will it bloom this year?
'Or has the sudden frost disturbed its bed?
'O keep the Dog far hence, that's friend to men,
'Or with his nails he'll dig it up again!'

Maneos counters:
''There I saw one I knew and stopped him, crying: 'Kolokotronis!'
'You whose ancestors fought bravely at Mycale and Thermopylae,
You whose sword triumphed at Tripolis,
And you who bled for Hellenic liberty.'
'Where are the others, the noble brothers of Hellas?'
'Has the Pasha passed through the mountain-pass?'
'How much longer will our supplies last?'
'No matter, I'll starve before I submit to the tyrannical fits
of the barbarian, Omer Vryonis,
Or the dictates of the dictator, Kioshe Mehmet:'
'For Zeus of the wide brows takes away one half of the virtue   67
from a man, once the day of slavery closes upon him.''

V

Eliot writes:
'In the juvescence of the year   68
Came Christ the tiger'

Maneos counters:
'In the juvescence of the year
Came Dionysus, of the wild mane, with his incense, his panthers, and
his leopards.'

Eliot writes:
'O Father we welcome your words,   69
And we will take heart for the future,
Remembering the past.

The heathen are come into thine inheritance,
And thy temple have they defiled.'

Maneos counters:
'O Zeus we welcome your words,
And we will take heart for the future,
Remembering our glorious past.

The Christians are come into thine inheritance
And thy temples have they defiled.'

Eliot writes:
'O lord, have patience   70
Pardon these derelictions -
I shall convince these romantic irritations
By my classical convictions.'

Maneos counters:
'O Zeus, have patience
Forgive this temporary lapse –
For I shall soon conquer this critical odyssey
With a renaissance of Romantic Beauty.'

Eliot writes:
'O weariness of men who turn from G O D   71
To the grandeur of your mind and the glory of your action,
To arts and inventions and daring enterprises,
To schemes of human greatness thoroughly discredited,'

Maneos counters:

'O to the daring of men who turn from the HOLY TRINITY
To the pleasures of the mind and to the pursuits of glory,
To arts, sciences, poetry and discovery,
To schemes of human inquiry and dreams of human divinity.'

Eliot writes:
'Sin is Behovely, but   72
All shall be well, and
All manner of thing shall be well.'

Maneos counters:
'Sin is lovely
as there is something
Godly about Ecstasy.
All shall be well
when I sing gloriously
in an Arcadian dell.'

Eliot writes:
'The Word of the LORD came unto me, saying: 73
O miserable cities of designing men,
O wretched generation of enlightened men'

Maneos counters:
'The Word of APOLLO, the far darter – came unto me, saying:
You are the one to lead the children of Hellas forth
You are the one to free the stolen North.'

Eliot writes:
'Son of Man, behold with thine eyes, and hear with thine ears 74
And set thine heart upon all that I show thee.'

Maneos counters:
'Oh Ares, Son of Zeus, please ease my fear of Hades.
Allow me to achieve elusive Aristos,
Here on these battle-fields of cypress-rich, Kypros.'

Eliot writes:
'O Lord, deliver me from the man of excellent intention and   75
impure heart: for the heart is deceitful above all things, and

desperately wicked.'

Maneos counters:
'Oh Julian – deliver me from the base Morality of Christianity.
Let Reason triumph over Mysticism
Hellenism over Galileanism
Beauty over Barbarism –
Where Attic Philosophy, like a battered Phoenix,
flies triumphantly over the twisted Crucifix.'

Eliot writes:
' But it seems that something has happened that has never hap-   76
    pened before: though we know not just when, or why, or
    how, or where.
Men have left GOD not for other gods, they say, but for no god;
  and this has never happened before'

Maneos counters:
'I couldn't agree more!
What's in store
for The West if we no longer have a soul, a core?
I have renounced the Galilean,
But at least, I worship the laurel, the palms, and the paean,
The breasts of the nymphs glistening in the ocean;

Yet some others, my brothers in Western Civilization, believe in
Nothing.
And I, Tiresias, can assure you of one thing,
that those who believe in Nothing
will be destroyed by enemies who believe in
Something, Anything!'

Eliot writes:
'Some were rapacious and lustful.   77
Many left their bodies to the kites of Syria
Or sea-strewn along the routes;
Many left their souls in Syria,
Living on, sunken in moral corruption;'

Maneos counters:

'I have swum in harems of fair-haired women
Immersing myself in the excesses of Sin –
And I can tell you with utter certainty
That there is no Epiphany found in Depravity
For Dissolution only breeds Disillusion.'

Eliot writes:
'And would it have been worth it, after all,   78
After the cups, the marmalade, the tea,
Among the porcelain, among some talk of you and me,
Would it have been worth while,
To have bitten off the matter with a smile,
To have squeezed the universe into a ball
To roll it toward some overwhelming question,
To say: "I am Lazarus, come from the dead,
Come back to tell you all, I shall tell you all" –'

Maneos counters:
'And would it have been worth it, after all,
After the poems, the arguments, and the bold Bacchanal calls –
Among the Hellenic porticoes, among spectacular speeches about the
glorious Greeks,
Would it have been worthwhile,
To have taunted the learned men of my age,
To have reviled the vile pages of the Christian sages,
And to have dressed my hair with wild sage,
Before pronouncing: 'I am Hypatia of Alexandria – come from the
dead,
Come back to tell you all, I shall tell you all.
Vicisti Galilaee   79
Sed anima Dios adhuc intra me vivit, Galilaee."

VI

Eliot writes:
'On Margate Sands.   80
I can connect
Nothing with nothing.
The broken fingernails of dirty hands.'

Maneos counters:
'On Amalfi sands
I can connect with everything:
The bird's singing, the Roman rings,
And the medieval kings.'

Eliot writes:
'Two ladies of uncertain age
Sit by a window drinking tea'
81

Maneos counters:
'Two young women of questionable age
Rest in the rotunda sipping Barbera'

Eliot writes:
'Under the brown fog of a winter dawn,
A crowd flowed over London Bridge, so many,
I had not thought death had undone so many.'
82

Maneos counters:
'Under The Tuscan Sun's glimmering glow
I tangled with *il veleno*
While dreaming of Morocco.'

Eliot writes:
'The readers of the Boston Evening Transcript
Sway in the wind like a field of ripe corn.'
83

Maneos counters:
'The readers of the Corriere della Sera
Sway in the quay like a sea of sea-kissed wheat.'

Eliot writes:
'I journeyed to London, to the timekept City,
Where the River flows, with foreign flotations.
There I was told: we have too many churches,
And too few chop-houses.'
84

Maneos counters:
'I journeyed to Rome, to The Eternal City,

Where the Tiber flows with Etruscan wine.
There I was told: *We have more beauty
here than anything found within poetry.*'

Eliot writes:
'Unreal City,
Under the brown fog of a winter dawn,
A crowd flowed over London Bridge, so many,
I had not thought death had undone so many.
Sighs, short and infrequent, were exhaled,
And each man fixed his eyes before his feet.
Flowed up the hill and down King William Street,
To where Saint Mary Woolnoth kept the hours
With a dead sound on the final stroke of nine.'

Maneos counters:
'Eternal City!
Under the shaded light of the fading moonlight,
A crowd streamed into Campo dei Fiori.
So many smiling faces, such a lovely sight.
Laughing, dancing, and kissing were now engaged in,
And each man contented himself in the company of companions.
Flowing up and down Via Giubbonari,
Into where Giordano Bruno defied the very papacy, what bravery!
And so, with a Romantic Roman sigh, I gladly joined the party.'

Eliot writes:
'Driven on the wind that sweeps the gloomy hills of London,   86
Hampstead and Clerkenwell, Campden and Putney,
Highgate, Primrose and Ludgate. Not here
Not here the darkness, in this twittering world.'

Maneos counters:
'Enjoying the joyous wind that sweeps through the sweet hills of
Rome,
Aventine and Caelian, Capitoline and Esquiline,
Palatine, Quirinal and Viminal. Here –
Here in this immortal light, in this delightful existence.'

Eliot writes:

'The eyes are not here 87
There are no eyes here
In this valley of dying stars
In this hollow valley
This broken jaw of our lost kingdoms

    In this last meeting places
We grope together
And avoid speech
Gathered on this beach of the tumid river'

Maneos counters:
'Our eyes meet
on this Roman street.
Under this valiant valley of pulsing stars
In this Eternal City
This poetic palace laced with marble and beauty.

In this most Romantic of meeting places
We kiss passionately, as if tomorrow we are destined for the ghastly
galleys:
Tasting the blood of past loves, the wine of our bodies.
We lie together, enraptured in rapturous uncertainty.'

Eliot writes:
'- Up a blind alley, stopped with broken walls 88
Papered with posters, chalked with childish scrawls! –'

Maneos counters:
'Strolling through the loggia, covered with rolling colors,
Contoured with Grecian figures:
Centaurs, satyrs, and minotaurs.'

Eliot writes:
'We have lingered in the chambers of the sea 89
By sea-girls wreathed with seaweed red and brown
Till human voices wake us, and we drown.'

Maneos counters:
'On this delicious day, we have forsaken *Arete* –

We have lingered in the Neapolitan bay
And here we will stay,
Lost in our dreamy play.'

Eliot writes:
'The Naming of Cats is a difficult matter,   90
It isn't just one of your holiday games;
You may think at first I'm mad as a hatter
When I tell you, a cat must have THREE DIFFERENT NAMES.'

Maneos counters:
'The Naming of glassy-eyed Concubines
is best done over a glass of Tuscan-splashed wine.
Especially, when you find them to be of the debauched kind.
You may say that I'm a miserable misogynist,
But actually, I'm a faithful philogynist.'

Eliot writes:
'HURRY UP PLEASE ITS TIME   91
HURRY UP PLEASE ITS TIME
Goodnight Bill. Goodnight Lou. Goodnight May. Goodnight.
Ta ta. Goodnight. Goodnight.'

Maneos counters:
'TAKE YOUR TIME WITH YOUR WINE
LET YOUR BODY AND MIND UNWIND
Ciao Michele. Ciao Stelio.'

Eliot writes:
'Sweet Thames, run softly till I end my song,   92
Sweet Thames, run softly, for I speak not loud or long.'

Maneos counters:
'Sweet Arno, flow softly till I end my tremulous trilling,
Sweet Arno, flow softly for I delight in your silk-soft singing.'

Eliot sings with Wagner:
'Frisch weht der Wind   93
Der Heimat zu
Mein Irisch Kind

Wo Weilest du?'

Maneos sings with Puccini:
'Chi son? Chi son? Son un poeta.   94
Che cosa faccio? Scrivo.
E come vivo? Vivo.
In poverta mia lieta
Scialo da gran signore
Rime ed inni d'amore.'

VII

Eliot writes:
'Webster was much possessed by death   95
And saw the skull beneath the skin;
And breastless creatures under ground
Leaned backwards with a lipless grin'

Maneos counters:
'Zorba was much possessed with Passion
when he witnessed the breathless beauty of dolphins.
He danced like a man entranced by Madness
Leaning backwards, eyes skyward, with an ecstatic grin,
Yasou Alexis!'

Eliot writes:
'PIPIT sate upright in her chair   96
Some distance from where I was sitting;
Views of the Oxford Colleges
Lay on the table, with the knitting.'

Maneos counters:
'CRISPINA, my wispy niece, sate upright in her chair
Some distance from where I was sitting;
Views of the Peloponnese
Lay on the table, along with her tomes on Greece.'

Eliot writes:
'I shall not want Honour in Heaven   97
For I shall meet Sir Phillip Sydney

And have talk with Coriolanus
And other heroes of that kidney.'

Maneos counters:
'I shall want Honor in Hades
For I shall meet fleet-footed, Diomedes,
Talk with hawkish, Achilles,
And converse with other Achaeans who once traversed the Aegean
Seas.'

Eliot writes:
'I shall not want Capital in Heaven   98
For I shall meet Sir Alfred Mond:
We two shall lie together, lapt
In a five per cent Exchequer Bond.'

Maneos counters:
'I shall not desire Modernism in Hell,
For I shall meet, Orpheus, the singing rebel.
I shall lie at his feet, weeping upon his sweet lyre,
As his wild songs swell like a hellish wildfire refusing to expire.'

Eliot writes:
'I shall not want Society in Heaven,   99
Lucretia Borgia shall be my Bride;
Her anecdotes will be more amusing
Than Pipit's experience could provide.'

Maneos counters:
'I shall not want morality in Hell,
For Lucrezia Borgia, the gorgeous paramour, shall be my exclusive
whore.
Her stately lips shall sate my insatiable tastes,
While her hips shall gyrate until I am bruised and sore.'

Eliot writes:
'I shall not want Pipit in Heaven: 100
Madame Blavatsky will instruct me
In the Seven Sacred Trances;
Piccarda de Donati will conduct me . . .'

Maneos counters:
'I shall not want Prufrock in Heaven:
Madame Skenderis, a Greek living in France, will instruct me
In the entrancing Zembekiko dance;
Mikis Theodorakis will conduct me. . .'

Eliot writes:
'When Mr. Apollinax visited the United States   101
His laughter tinkled among the teacups.
I thought of Fragilion, that shy figure among the birch-trees,
And of Priapus in the shrubbery
Gaping at the lady in the swing.'

Maneos counters:
'When Signora Da Vinci visited the United States
Her boisterous laughter ruptured the teacups.
I thought of Lucrezia Borgia, the Papal princess,
And of Dido, burning upon her pyre for callous Aeneas,
Writhing in severe agony like the tearful soul of Miss Maria Callas.'

Eliot writes:
'I Tiresias, though blind, throbbing between two lives,   102
Old man with wrinkled female breasts, can see
At the violet hour, the evening hour that strives
Homeward, and brings the sailor home from the sea.'

Maneos counters:
'I Achilles, though wounded still possess the breast of peerless Ares.
As I strut between the Achaeans and the Myrmidons,
I exhort my men to make quick sport of the cohorts led by Priam's
prized sons.
For I refuse to retreat to the sweet pleasures of pleasant Aphrodite, the
goddess of the sweet-flowing seas.'

Eliot writes:
'I Tiresias, old man with wrinkled dugs   103
Perceived the scene, and foretold the rest –
I too awaited the expected guest.
He, the young man carbuncular, arrives

A small house agent's clerk, with one bold stare,
One of the low on whom assurance sits
As a silk hat on a Bradford millionaire.'

Maneos counters:
'I, me, *Pietros Maneos de la Mancha*, a young man with exceeding
Passion
Challenge you, the son of Xerxes, Ahmadinejad,
to a gladiatorial fight in the mighty mountains of Thermopylae
or in the holy landscape of Tempe:
Pitting the Free against those who propagate Tyranny!
Hand to hand, chest to chest, eye to eye combat before God
Fought bitterly, savagely, to the very End!'

Eliot writes:
'Miss Nancy Ellicott 104
Strode across the hills and broke them,
Road across the hills and broke them—
The barren New England hills—
Riding to hounds
Over the cow-pasture.

Miss Nancy Ellicott smoked
And danced all the modern dances;
And her aunts were not quite sure how they felt about it,
But they knew that it was modern.'

Maneos counters:
'Gaius Julius Caesar
Strode across the Gallic hills and conquered them,
Road across the bucolic hills and conquered them.
The barren barbarian hills were no match for conquering Caesar.

In Outer Gaul, Caesar seized immortal glory.
His peers feared his kingly ambitions,
But the plebeians endorsed and adored his regal visions.

So now, let all of Rome and all of the known world proclaim:
Here in Gaul, the God Caesar, trod over mere men.'

VIII

Eliot writes:
'This music is successful with a "dying fall"   105
Now that we talk of dying -
And should I have the right to smile?'

Maneos counters:
'This fornicating is successful with a 'lively rhythm'
Now that we are intensely alive
Do I have any right to brood over death?'

Eliot writes:
'So here I am, in the middle way, having had twenty years   106
Twenty years largely wasted, the years of l'entre deux guerres
Trying to learn to use words, and every attempt
Is a wholly new start, and a different kind of failure
Because one has only learnt to get the better of words.'

Maneos counters:
'So here I am, in the middle way, having had twenty-two years –
Twenty-two years largely wasted, the years of misplaced love
Trying to be beloved, yet every attempt
Is a lonely new start, and a different kind of failure
Because one has only mastered the art of fleeting pleasure.'

Eliot writes:
'You will write, at any rate.   107
Perhaps it is not too late.
I shall sit here, serving tea to friends.'

Maneos counters:
'She has not written, at any rate.
Perhaps she is content with her new mate.
I shall sit here, singing the Rembetic blues, and drinking ouzo.'

Eliot writes:
'I am always sure that you understand   108
My feelings, always sure that you feel,
Sure that across the gulf you reach your hand.'

Maneos counters:
'Although she is with another,
I am still sure that she understands my pained soul,
Still sure that she hears my naked voice breaking upon the shimmering shoal.'

Eliot writes:
'No doubt, an easy tool,   109
Deferential, glad to be of use,
Politic, cautious, and meticulous;
Full of high sentence, but a bit obtuse
At times, indeed, almost ridiculous --
Almost, at times, the Fool.'

Maneos counters:
'Without a doubt, a difficult man –
Mad, bad and dangerous to know:
Or is that pose merely for show?
Nevertheless, more infamous than famous,
Political, Pontifical and Heretical;
Full of raving prophecies, yet hardly theoretical.
At times, the whining fool,
Yet always, the one with the bold plan.'

Eliot writes:
'the creation of a work of art is like some other forms of creation,   110
a painful and unpleasant business; it is a sacrifice of the man to the work,
it is a kind of death.'

Maneos counters:
'There's a whore on my right
And she'll be here all night
Even when I begin to write
Under the glorious Italian moon-light.'

Eliot writes:
'Co co rico co co rico'   111

Maneos counters:

'Aman! Aman! Amannnnnn!'

Eliot writes:
'Now Albert's coming back, make yourself a bit smart.   112
He'll want to know what you done with that money he gave you
To get yourself some teeth. He did, I was there.
You have them all out, Lil, and get a nice set,
He said, I swear, I can't bear to look at you.
And no more can't I, I said, and think of poor Albert,
He's been in the army four years, he wants a good time,
And if you don't give it to him, there's others will, I said.'

Maneos counters:
'Do you really believe that we can vanquish the English?
They are much stronger than us.
Our band of irregulars will surely be crushed.
Perhaps, but it is not only a question of possibility, but also of duty.
I agree with Hamilton – better to die free than live in slavery.
Don't tread on me!
I like the ring of that, my boy!
And I would even go so far as to exclaim,
Let the English kill any man they find
without weapons of any kind!'

Eliot writes:
'Bolo's big black bastard queen   113
Was so obscene
She shocked the folk of Golder's Green.'

Maneos counters:
'Jean Verdenal, the dashing Frenchman
Was so handsome
That he made Mr. Eliot numb
and even possibly.......'

Eliot writes:
'In the room the women come and go   114
Talking of Michelangelo.'

Maneos counters:

'In the room the women come and go
Gushing over Samo.'

Eliot writes:
'I an old man,   115
A dull head among windy spaces. . .'

Maneos counters:
'I, me, a young man –
A burning soul among mannered mandarins. . .'

Eliot writes:
'I have measured out my life with coffee spoons;'   116

Maneos counters:
'My life has been absent any measure
But rich in earthly pleasure:
Full of wonderful wanderings –
The flowing blood of flowing-haired Kings
The honey-tinged singing of sin-bringing Sirens,
And the bloody homecoming into Ithakan glens.'

Eliot writes:
'Shall I say it again? In order to arrive there,   117
To arrive where you are, to get from where you are not,
  You must go by a way wherein there is no ecstasy.'

Maneos counters:
'Shall I say it again?
I am not merely a poet of Ecstasy, Odysseus.
I am Ecstasy incarnate!
A modern Bacchus
(Or is it Icarus?),
awash in hubris,
taunting the vaunted Fates
by flying to the very gates
of the Sun.'

Eliot writes:
'Do I dare   118

Disturb the universe?'

Maneos counters:
'*L'univers c'est moi!*'

Eliot writes:
'I smile, of course,   119
And go on drinking tea.'

Maneos counters:
'Amidst the Prufrockian clatter and chatter from within
I quietly hymn Pierian-hymns into the wide, wild wind.'

Eliot writes:
'I shall sit here, serving tea to friends. . . ."   120

Maneos counters:
'I shall sit here, sullen and solitary,
lost in my Grecian fantasy. . . .
I shall need not yet three
to make a new Thermopylae.
Merely, just you and me!'

Eliot writes:
'I grow old. . . I grow old. . .   121
I shall wear the bottoms of my trousers rolled.'

Maneos counters:
'I too grow old,
But I shall *never* wear the bottoms of my trousers rolled!'

IX

Eliot writes:
'Life departs with a feeble smile   122
Into the indifferent.'

Maneos counters:
'Life departs with an impassioned kiss
Into the everlasting abyss.'

Eliot writes:
'Man's life is powerless and brief and dark   123
It is not possible for me to make her happy.'

Maneos counters:
'Oh to exclamatory ecstasy!
It is certainly possible for me to make her happy!'

Eliot writes:
'There is no relief but in grief   124
O when will the creaking heart cease?
When will the broken chair give ease?
Why will the summer day delay?
When will Time flow away?'

Maneos counters:
'There is some relief in but a brief moment of Beauty –
A baby's shy smile
A perfectly crafted simile
A mere glimpse of dazzling Daphne, resting solemnly,
Under the flowering laurel tree.'

Eliot writes:
'O dark dark dark. They all go into the dark,   125
The vacant interstellar spaces, the vacant into the vacant,
The captains, merchant bankers, eminent men of letters,'

Maneos counters:
'O light, light, light! Some do not go gently into the eternal night
Verily, some sneer at death's eerie sight
The saints, the madmen, and the poets,'

Eliot concludes with a whimper:
'This is the way the world ends   126
This is the way the world ends
This is the way the world ends
Not with a bang but a whimper.'

Maneos concludes with a dance:

'This is the way the world ends
This is the way the world ends
This is the way the world ends
Not with a resigned whimper, but rather, a wild, whirling dance!'

X

In Bukowski there is very little poetry.
But this vulgar hack has hacked his way into literary fame.
More of a *Barfly* than a bard –
Yet, his is now a celebrated name.
Have the literati no shame?

Bukowski slobbers:
'what a world, you think: eat, work, fuck,
die.'

    127

Maneos composes:
'What a world, you think!
The Grecian dancers,
The Italian gardens,
The Tunisian light
And the Parisian lovers.

What a world, you think!
The symphonies of Mozart,
The sonnets of Shakespeare,
The frescoes of Fra Angelico,
And the selfless suffering of Christ.'

Bukowski slobbers:
'think of the beds
used again and again
to fuck in
to die in.'

    128

Maneos composes:
'Think of the beds
used again and again
to consummate the consuming love
between two lovers.'

Bukowski slobbers:
'if I bet on Humanity
I'd never cash a ticket.'

    129

Maneos composes:
'I'd bet on Humanity
Even if 'wise society'
Mocked my naivety.'

Bukowski slobbers:
'humanity
you sick
motherfucker.'

130

Maneos composes:
'humanity –
as resilient
as the scents of spring,
or the storms of the storied sea.'

Bukowski slobbers:
'barbaric, senseless days total
in your skull;
reality is a juiceless
orange.'

131

Maneos composes:
'Aesthetic, Passionate days tally
in your Soul.
Reality is a bruised daisy.'

Bukowski slobbers:
'there is no god
there are no politics
there is no peace
there is no love'

132

Maneos composes:
'I Hope for a God
I Hope for a less divisive Political discourse
I Hope for Peace
I Love.'

Bukowski slobbers:
'then one day   133
we heard
a voice
from the house
"YOU GOD DAMNED
WHORE!"'

Maneos composes:
'Then one day
We overheard her young lover say
Beneath the richly-wreathed moon
You are as Beautiful as a Rose
in full bloom.'

Bukowski slobbers:
'but I caught her and   134
grabbed at the bottle.
"give me that bottle, you
fucking whore!"'

Maneos composes:
'But I pinned her
against the dresser,
Give me a thousand kisses
then a thousand more,
and then a thousand on top of this –
as many kisses as there are wisps of sand
in the wind-kissed Kalahari.'

Bukowski slobbers:
'what a whore.   135
what a hunk of rock.'

Maneos composes:
'What a Goddess!
An empress blessed with twirling tresses
Whose bronzed flesh is so luscious
that I am delirious –
Delirious as a drunken Satyr dancing with Bacchus:

Flushed with both Ecstasy and Agony:
Crushed with Passion, Paralyzed with Lust, truly,
A beautiful tragedy, a sweet-bitter reality.
For my longings, my sufferings, will be the death of me!'

Bukowski slobbers:
"YOU GOD DAMNED WHORE,
WHAT DO YOU KNOW ABOUT
ANYTHING?
SITTING THERE ON YOUR
DEAD ASS AND
SUCKING AT THE VINO!"

136

Maneos composes:
'I ache for your kisses!
Like a dying well for a single drop of water
Like a starving beggar for a single scrap of silver
Like a weeping Tragedy for a single note of laughter.

I want to mark your skin with the sins of Passion!'

Bukowski slobbers:
'it was all right with me, I didn't want to be
liked by them, I didn't want to fuck them or
marry them or
even date them.
I found none of them
Beautiful.'

137

Maneos composes:
'My lovely butterfly,
you are a Renaissance of Beauty.
Can I close
your wild, wild eyes
with kisses of wild rose?'

Bukowski slobbers:
'girls remind me of hair in the sink, girls remind me of intestines
and bladders and excretory movements; it's unfortunate also that
ice-cream bells, babies, engine-valves, plagiostomes, palm trees,

138

footsteps in the hall . . . all excite me with the cold calmness
of the gravestone;'

Maneos composes:
'Girls remind me of diaphanous diamonds
Of dew and fire bejeweled with forgotten Grecian-garlands –
Of limb-loosening singing drifting in
from the low-lying woodlands.

It's also fortunate that ice-cream, babies, forests, and glens
all excite me with the same impassioned intensity of an inviting glance
from a full beautiful maiden.'

Bukowski slobbers:
'I'm glad I got to them   139
all, I'm glad I got so many of them
in.

I flipped them
poked them
gored them.

so many high-heeled shoes
under my bed
it looked like a January
Clearance Sale.'

Maneos composes:
'I've been with 'this one' and 'that one.'
Fair-haired models, delicious jezebels
and even demure southern belles.
Contessas, marchesas, and principessas
have all conveniently forgotten their virtue
when in my fleshy purview.
Starlets and harlots alike have taken their pleasure,
and even the twin daughters of a Roman butcher
have knelt at my illicit altar.
And if you're reading this while in bed
with your significant other –
slightly turn your head,

for it's likely that I've been with 'that one' too.'

Bukowski slobbers:
"ah, jam it up   140
your ass!" she
screamed at
me.'

Maneos composes:
"Ravage me with kisses,'
She panted in between caresses,
like a panther exiled in an exotic jungle.'

XI

Bukowski slobbers:
'waiting for death   141
like a cat
that will jump on the
bed'

Maneos composes:
'Tearing the nectar from Life
Like a hyena high on blood and bone.'

Bukowski slobbers:
'tricked and slugged to   142
zero
they wait on death
with the temperate patience of
a mother teaching her child
to eat:'

Maneos composes:
'Resplendent and transfigured by transcendent Emotion
They embrace Life
With the Passion and Desperation
Of a Lion on the verge of Starvation
Chasing a wild-eyed wildebeest
Despairing for a restorative Feast.'

Bukowski slobbers:
'waiting
in a life full of little stories
for a death to come'

Maneos composes:
'Sometimes, I wish I were a wild petunia.
Lost in the hidden singing of a golden savanna –
Blossoming for but a single spring morning:
A morning of pure Beauty, pure Glory.
Far superior to a long life exiled amidst The Ugly.
For Beauty is not only Truth
But the very proof of Divinity.'

Bukowski slobbers:
'there's
all that time
to eat
drink
and
wait on death
like
everybody
else.'

Maneos composes:
'There's simply not enough Time
To drink every carafe of wine,
Satisfy every longing of the mind,
Or bed every willing concubine.

But one can still embrace every
Ember of Life, tasting every available Sensation
Before facing Death with utter Hubris,
that the golden Gods of Olympus
are both impressed and astonished.'

Bukowski slobbers:
'all that really mattered was

going someplace
the faster the better
because it left less waiting
to die.'

Maneos composes:
'all that really matters is
to feel alive,
if only for a single moment –
to feel in Intense Sensation
that our existence is not an endless repetition
of sleeping, eating, drinking, and dressing.'

Bukowski slobbers:
'very well. grant us this moment: standing before a mirror   146
in my dead father's suit
waiting also
to die.'

Maneos composes:
'If the Gods have any sympathy,
they will pity me.
For they have already taken my Father,
while my mother breathes through a ventilator.
How much horror can a man endure?'

Bukowski slobbers:
'death is not a problem; waiting around for it   147
is.'

Maneos composes:
'Oh, if only it were 1821!
To once again defend Grecian Freedom –
To fight alongside Byron,
against the haughty Ottomans,
forever ending foreign dominion!

Oh, if only it were 1821!
To fight under the Apollonian sun versus the occupying Barbarians –

To stand defiantly, with the sons of Olympians, the scions of
Athenians
To die upon my shield like a Spartan!

Oh, if only it were 1821, we'd fight like the Heroes from Roumeli
… You'd see …
We'd push the Turkish garrisons into the Sea
For we Hellenes are destined to be Free –

But alas,
It is 1974, nearing the terminus of the 20th century,
so instead of battling boldly
we all flee ignominiously
from the tyranny of the Turkish lash!'

Bukowski slobbers:
'it is a bad place to die;   148
any place is a bad place to die,'

Maneos composes:
'Nicosia would be a perfect place to perish –
For I can imagine nothing more Glorious
Than resisting the Turkish presence in Cyprus
In the name of ancient Hellas!'

Bukowski slobbers:
'
            Keats is dead   149
        and I am dying too.'

Maneos composes:
'Beauty lasts for Eternity
And with each passing Century
It becomes more Lovely.
So you see, Mr. Bukowski,
Despite the very best efforts of the Quarterly
Keats will never pass into obscurity.
Though the same cannot be said of you or your 'Poetry!''

XII

Bukowski slobbers:
'I do not like the human race.
I don't like their heads.
I don't like their faces.
I don't like their feet.
I don't like their conversations.
I don't like their hairdos.
I don't like their automobiles.
I don't like their dogs, or their cats,
Or their roses.'

Maneos composes:
'I despise Society
and it me.
The feeling is mutual
as it should be.
But this is not a manifestation
of chic nihilism
so much as impassioned pastoralism.

I much prefer the unexplored haunts of Nature
to the crowded confines of a city.
For the noxious and obnoxious chatter
emanating from a polluted polis
poisons one's soul with its menial, mindless palaver.
Yet, the glories of a sprawling pasture
painted in crepuscular amber –
A glistening mountain spring
singing in a forgotten valley –
Or a faint glimpse of a cardinal's wing
glimmering in the distant wind
send the senses into a whirlwind
of soul-pleasing pleasure.

For to wander lonely as a cloud
or for that matter
a proud, pastoral deity
waving his thyrsus
with Dionysus
is pure, pagan Ecstasy.

And to hear the dried, dying
leaves crackle beneath one's feet
on an aimless odyssey
through Wilkes County
is sweet
as a symphony of similes
swimming in dripping streams of honey.'

Bukowski slobbers:
'I stayed another week   151
painted her a couple of good paintings
one of a man being hanged
and another of a woman being fucked by a wolf.'

Maneos composes:
'I stayed another week
And painted her a couple of Baroque paintings:

One of morose Moroccan pirates raiding an Italian brigade,
And another of Antony dying in the arms of his charming lover,
Cleopatra:
'And if he'd fallen now, he hadn't fallen humbly   152
but as a Roman vanquished by a Roman.''

Bukowski slobbers:
'maybe she   153
fucks the rosebuds
and finches
before she writes
her poems'

Maneos composes:
'Maybe she
kisses the cyclamen
and the jasmine
before writing her short stories'

Bukowski slobbers:
' it was a splendid day in Spring   154

and outside we could hear the birds
        that hadn't been killed
                by the smog'

Maneos composes:
'It was a splendid Spring morning
As we listened to the regal trilling
Of the forlorn nightingale
Regaling his former Lover with lovely spring-singing.'

Bukowski slobbers:
'The moon looks   155
diseased

my hands slip
on the
steering wheel'

Maneos composes:
'The moon looks
as radiant as a brook
afire with magma
and acacia.

Under the Roman sky, my fingers tenderly caress Constantine's arch:
And as the dreamy lovers march by, I let out a sighing cry –
For I wish to remain here in Rome until I die.'

Bukowski slobbers:
'the moonlight always seemed fake   156
to me, maybe it was,'

Maneos composes:
'The moonlight always seemed holy
to me, maybe it was'

Bukowski slobbers:
'I wanna be like George Raft, I   157
thought.'

Maneos composes:
'I want to be like Antinous or Spartacus, I thought:
Living Art or a Living Hero.'

Bukowski slobbers:
'I'm Chopin, drunk, clutching my Polack soul,
the last bad man,'

158

Maneos composes:
'I'm Chatterton, drunk, clutching arsenic
Wondering whether to take a sip
of the fateful drink.'

Bukowski slobbers:
'it hasn't told us
about the gutters
or the suicides.

159

or the terror of one person
aching in one place
alone

untouched
unspoken to

watering a plant.'

Maneos composes:
'it hasn't told us
About the Tuscan snowdrops,
The sonorous songs sung in Missolonghi,
Or the hopping twilight trembling in the light-filled hills of Thessaly.

It has shunned the tales of the terrible Huns,
Avoided heavenly African gales,
And paled at sweaty erotic fun.'

Bukowski slobbers:
'there he is:
not too many hangovers

160

not too many fights with women
not too many flat tires
never a thought of suicide'

Maneos composes:
'there he is, Charles Bukowski:
too many hangovers
too many fights with women
too many bad poems
bi-polar and suicidal.'

Bukowski slobbers:
'why is it that the pickup truck   161
carrying the loose refrigerator
on the freeway
is always going between
80 and 90 m.p.h.?'

Maneos composes:
'Why is it that women
always quiver when I bite
their lower lip?'

Bukowski slobbers:
'Or the time they found the Jap nurse in the shell-hole   162
who had been hit in the breast and wanted some sulfa
and one of the boys said, "Hey, you think we can fuck
her before she dies?"'

Maneos composes:
'Or the time the nurse saved the dying patient
by donating a dangerous amount of her own blood.'

'Do you remember her words?'

'Yes, I do.'

'Even if I faint, take as much blood as you need."

XIII

Bukowski slobbers:
'as a very young man I divided an equal amount of time between   163
the bars and the libraries;'

Maneos composes:
'As a very young man I divided an equal amount of time between
the gymnasiums and the bookstores.'

Bukowski slobbers:
'in the bars, I thought I was a tough, I broke things, fought   164
other men, etc.'

Maneos composes:
'In the gymnasia, I thought I was a Greek God, I oiled myself, flexed
in the mirror, etc.
Was I Narcissus, Antinous, or Bacchus?'

Bukowski slobbers:
'I am not infected with ambition   165
I am quite content;'

Maneos composes:
'I am plagued with incurable ambition,
which is why I'm an incorrigible malcontent.'

Bukowski slobbers:
'but almost   166
at once
(as such things occur)
the lady I loved dearly
took off
and began to
fuck
around the clock
with
male and female
strangers
imbeciles
and (to be fair)

probably with some fairly
decent folk.'

Maneos composes:
'The lady that I loved truly, dearly, sincerely
left me because she couldn't overcome her crumbling Love
for her former Lover.
So here I am, with fragments of poems, fragments of kisses,
and fragments of Love.'

Bukowski slobbers:
'I lifted my drink and thought about   167
lighting a cigarette.'

Maneos composes:
'I lifted my drink
and thought about
my wasted passion.'

Bukowski slobbers:
'   I   168
no longer
read
I
no longer
breed,
I
talk to old men over quiet
fences.'

Maneos composes:
'One hungry nymph within sight
And another sinning plaything to my right.
I just might
find the fight
to add a third to these Bacchic Rites:
A veritable *menage a quatre*
How many more can I devour today?'

Bukowski slobbers:

"your poems about the girls will still be around
50 years from now when the girls are gone,"
my editor phones me.'

169

Maneos composes:
"Your poems will still be around
500 years from now, when you and I are deep in the ground,'
my editor tells me.'

Bukowski slobbers:
'I have been getting letters from a young poet

170

(very young, it seems) telling me that some day
I will most surely be recognized as
one of the world's great poets. *Poet!*'

Maneos composes:
'I keep receiving letters from a young PhD candidate
proclaiming that I am America's greatest poet.
Yet he doesn't believe that my Genius will be appreciated
until a much later date.'

Bukowski slobbers:
'I'M A GENIUS AND NOBODY KNOWS IT BUT

171

ME!'

Maneos composes:
'I'M A GENIUS AND NOBODY KNOWS IT BUT
ME!'

XIV

Bukowski slobbers:
'she lives on a side street somewhere

172

in Glendale
and I help him unfold the
roadmap as we sip our
diet Schlitz.'

Maneos composes:
'She lives on a side street inside the center of Testaccio.

67

She's here in Rome to study the appearance of
The Classical Aesthetic throughout the ages.'

Bukowski slobbers:
'I rented a 6 dollar a week   173
room
in Chinatown
with a window as large as the
side of the world'

Maneos composes:
'I rented a six thousand dollar a week
room
in Rome's Piazza Navona
with an Athenaeum as large as several suburban homes.'

Bukowski slobbers:
'I keep remembering the horses   174
under the moon
I keep remembering feeding the horses
sugar
white oblongs of sugar
more like ice,'

Maneos composes:
'I keep remembering Rome
under the September-moon
I keep remembering the frescoes
in Pompeii;

vivid reds the color of gushing blood exposing ancient stories.'

Bukowski slobbers:
'   today I walked in the sun and streets   175
of this city: seeing nothing, learning nothing, being
nothing, and coming back to my room
I passed an old woman who smiled a horrible smile;
she was already dead, and everywhere I remembered wires:'

Maneos composes:

'This afternoon, after a glorious tryst, I walked *Under The Roman Sun*
through various venues, Via Cavour, Via dei Fori Imperali
with the imperium of Trajan:
Endeavoring to savor everything: the lore, the aromas, the colors.
I passed a young woman whose smile was of poppies and honey –
Who was so intensely alive, possessing such vim and vitality,
That I longed to throw myself upon her
like a honeybee uncovering undiscovered nectar.'

Bukowski slobbers:
'in the morning when I went to turn in my key
I asked the lady, 'by the way, could you tell me
which way I go to get to L.A.?''

"you're in L.A.," she told me.'

Maneos composes:
'In the morning when I went to turn in my key
I asked the lady, 'by the way, could you tell me
which way I go to get to Umbria?'

'You're in Umbria,' she told me.'

Bukowski slobbers:
'it was one of those hot and tiring days at Hollywood
Park
with a huge crowd, a
tiring, rude, dumb
crowd.'

Maneos composes:
'it was one of those sun-running summer afternoons in Florence
with a huge crowd teeming
into Piazza della Signoria like a running stream from some forgotten
dream:
Wide-eyed, doe-eyed, dove-eyed.'

Bukowski slobbers:
"hey! where the hell
you going?"

"I'm going to the fucking
bar!"

Maneos composes:
"Hey there! Where are you going today?'

'I'm going alone into the Coliseum
to fight Ahmadinejad, the Persian,
in single combat, *sine missione*!"

Bukowski slobbers:
'I pay, ask him directions   179
to Beverly Hills and drive off
into the sick drooping
pink sun.'

Maneos composes:
'I thank the two nuns
before asking them for directions
into a historical section.
I drive off into the thriving Italian sun!'

Bukowski slobbers:
'pink sun pink sun   180
I hate your holiness'

Maneos composes:
'Wild, unbridled Sun! A burning hoplon of Apollonian allure!
I am hypnotized by your hypnotic, exotic color:
As if soft-mauve and burnt-orange fell deeply and passionately in
Love –
giving birth to each succeeding beam of light streaming
into the ocean –
that brilliant mirror whose reflections
reveal the very thoughts of the Olympians.'

Bukowski slobbers:
'I watch the old ladies   181
in the supermarket,

angry and alone.'

Maneos composes:
'I watch the old ladies
in the piazza,
gesturing and laughing.'

Bukowski slobbers:
'I figured the town was finally getting   182
to me
and about a week later I
hopped a Greyhound to
Philly.'

Maneos composes:
'I figured this country
was truly stifling me
so I escaped to serene Sicily.'

Bukowski slobbers:
'there's nothing quite like driving the   183
hairpin curves on the Pasadena Freeway at 85
m.p.h.
hung over'

Maneos composes:
'There's nothing quite like swerving around the
hairpin curves in Positano on a sumptuous summer night:
I think that even in my dreams I shall never forget it.'

Bukowski slobbers:
'hanging from the doorknob   184
is an ad from the All American
Burger
consisting of several coupons'

Maneos composes:
'Hanging from a gilded doorknob
is an ad for Verdi's *Il Corsaro*

consisting of florid reds splashed beneath the dashing Pirate.
VIVA CORRADO!'

Bukowski slobbers:
'to sit in a small room   185
and drink a can of beer
and roll a cigarette
while listening to Brahms
on a small red radio'

Maneos composes:
'to sit in an expansive Piazza
and drink expensive wine
and devour linguine
while listening to Puccini
being performed by a stormy gypsy.'

Bukowski slobbers:
'you think about how   186
you once decided to be buried
near Hollywood Park
so you could hear the horses pound by
as you slept'

Maneos composes:
'you think about how
you once decided to have your ashes placed
in one of Bernini's fountains in Piazza Navona,
so that you could watch the endless stream of lovers
stroll through the piazza sharing kisses and gelato, endlessly.'

Bukowski slobbers:
'I believe the thought came to me   187
when I was about eleven years
old:
        I'll become an idiot.'

Maneos composes:
'I believe the thought came to me
when I was in Piazza Cavour, or maybe it

was in Piazza del Gesu:
I'll become a Poet!'

Bukowski slobbers:
'you should have seen that place in Philly, just 2 dollars a week,   188
she said, and it was up under the attic
roof.
just what I need, I thought, I can live here FOREVER and
KREE-ATE.'

Maneos composes:
'You should have seen Villa Lamaro in Sorrento.
It's five thousand dollars a week, but you'll be happy, she said.
Just what I need I thought.
I could live here forever, staring at the Neapolitan light,
Writing about these picturesque sights.'

Bukowski slobbers:
'they go inside and it begins   189
to rain as
3 gun shots sound half a block
away and
one of the skyscrapers in
downtown L.A. begins
burning
25 foot flames licking toward
doom.'

Maneos composes:
'The group went inside IL GESU to hide from the incipient rain.
Faintly, in the distance, they heard IL TROVATORE
being sung by four Romanian gypsies.
Although, the rain was beginning to change into snow,
they all left the church in search of the impassioned singers.'

Bukowski slobbers:
'she was sitting in the window   190
of room 1010 at the Chelsea
in New York,
Janis Joplin's old room.

It was 104 degrees
and she was on speed
and had one leg over
the sill,'

Maneos composes:
'This was the first time that the Marchioness
had visited the Keats-Shelley House
in Rome's hallowed Piazza di Spagna.
In the very room where John expired,
she was inspired
to read the whole
of 'Sleep and Poetry' to Keats' Orphic soul.'

Bukowski slobbers:
'but I still knew (despite my 2-bit cheap insanity)   191
that there was an awful lot of bad writing out there being
called great, which really was no better than what I could
do under that Philly roof'

Maneos composes:
'but I still knew (despite my monstrous egotism)
that there was an awful lot of bad writing out there
winning awards, which was really no better than I
could do on this sun-kissed balcony in Sorrento.'

Bukowski slobbers:
'sometimes a man has to take refuge in   192
a motel room
to save his
god-damned soul.'

Maneos composes:
'Sometimes a man has to take refuge in
a timeless Palazzo to rejuvenate his time-worn soul.'

Bukowski slobbers:
'Hemingway said, "it won't come   193
anymore."
later - the gun

into the
mouth."

Maneos composes:
'Caesar said, 'I've got you, Africa!'
Later – the glorious triumphs in Rome.'

Bukowski slobbers:
'   and   194
nobody speaks of the
hills of Rome
anymore.'

Maneos composes:
'From atop the sun-suffused summit of the Janiculum hill (Piazzale del
Gianicolo),
the two Belgium lovers admired the lovely view of glorious Rome;
they swore to each other that somehow they would make this their new
home.'

Bukowski slobbers:
'it all ended   195
some place, somewhere,
in a small
room in downtown L.A.'

Maneos composes:
'it all ended
some place, somewhere
in a small
piazza in central Calabria.'

XV

Bukowski slobbers:
'I decided never to become an American.   196
my hero was Baron Manfred von Richthofen
the German air ace;'

Maneos composes:

'I decided never to acquiesce to American mass culture.
my hero was Alexis Zorba,
the modern Dionysus.'

Bukowski slobbers:
'I'd even like to visit   197
Andernach, Germany, the place where
I began. then I'd like to
fly on to Moscow'

Maneos composes:
'I'd like to see
the city of my ancestors,
Mytilene, Lesbos,
explore it,
then fly on to
Paphos.'

Bukowski slobbers:
'the guy in the front court can't   198
speak English, he's Greek, a
rather stupid-looking and
fairly ugly man.'

Maneos composes:
'the guy in the front court can't
speak English, for he's a Greek; he has a defiant brow
and a Homeric scowl.'

Bukowski slobbers:
'I called the waiter over and I said,   199
I think I am going to turn this table over, I'm
bored, I'm insane, I need
action, call in your goon, I'll piss on his
collarbone.'

Maneos composes:
'I called the waiter over and I said,
I'm going to dance on this table, I'm
restless, I'm insane.

I need to release my madness, so turn on burning Terzis,
And have your louts hold the table, so that
I'm able to move about like the God that I am.'

Bukowski slobbers:
'while drunk
I fingerfuck this 19 year old groupie
in bed with me.'

200

Maneos composes:
'While drunk,
I dance the bold Kalamatiano
with this wizened old monk.'

Bukowski slobbers:
'you're a beast, she said
your big white belly
and those hairy feet.'

201

Maneos composes:
"You're a Greek God,' she said –
'Your bulging biceps,
and your chiseled chest."

Bukowski slobbers:
'I let myself dream. I dream of
being famous. I dream of
walking the streets of London and
Paris. I dream of
sitting in cafes
drinking fine wines and
taking a taxi back to a good
Hotel.'

202

Maneos composes:
'I let myself dream.
I dream of being Alexander or a Spartan commander.
I dream of dancing in the Theban hills with Dionysus,
And prancing in Athens with Theseus.'

Bukowski slobbers:
'I dreamed I drank an Arrow shirt
and stole a broken
pail'

204

Maneos composes:
'I dream that I somehow can advance
the ideal of Eleutheria
in Tehran, Damascus, or Nicosia –
be it with the written word or the brazen sword.'

Bukowski slobbers:
'I wish I were driving a blue 1952 Buick
Or a dark blue 1942 Buick
Or a blue 1932 Buick
Over a cliff of hell and into the
sea.'

204

Maneos composes:
'I wish I were visiting Sparta, of the beautiful women:
I would swim in the Eurotas, of the thin-limbs,
while the feminine gems of Lacedaemon,
danced in Dionysian fashion:
Ambrosial Nights filled with garlands, kissing and sin!'

Bukowski slobbers:
'I need a haircut,
wonder what happened to
Blaze O'Brien the one-eyed
dentist?
if I open the closet door there'll
be a severed head in
there.'

205

Maneos composes:
'I wonder what happened to
Leonidas, the bravest of the Hellenes.
If I open that closet door,
will Xerxes be feasting upon his spleen?'

Bukowski slobbers:
'Helen! Helen! where are you?   206
damned woman, probably down-
stairs making pots of fudge.'

Maneos composes:
'Helen! Helen! Where are you?
Damned woman, you would have
us all be slaves
just so you can lay with your princely knave.'

Bukowski slobbers:
'there are no heroes,   207
there is only a mouse
in the corner
blinking its eyes,'

Maneos composes:
'Then Hephaistion, of the swift feet, lifted his spear to face the
oncoming Lycian horde. His face glistened like a God, as he prepared
to deal dark death to the hated enemy. Yet before he could strike the
fierce Lycians, an errant arrow pierced his breast-plate; he collapsed
into the cold mud. As the life ebbed from his limbs, he thought of his
home in rugged Aigilips, and his dear wife – alone – plying her distaff.
His tears and his blood puddled within his shield, forming a river of
Tragedy, a stream of fallen dreams.

And so fell Hephaistion, most beautiful of the Hellenes.'

Bukowski slobbers:
'   the dark is empty;   208
most of our heroes have been
            wrong'

Maneos composes:
'The burnished beams of light stream into the room like thin
strands of threaded gold.
And as dawn with her golden robe disrobes upon the distant horizon,
I gaze into the Sun,
And begin to sing of Proud Heroes, Ancient and Modern,

Grecian and Barbarian.
From those who fell in the plains of Plataea
To those Seals chosen to send Osama
To his final, fitting end.'

Bukowski slobbers:
'   nobody   209
wins. ask
Caesar.'

Maneos composes:
'Ha! Tell that to Alexander!'

XVI

Bukowski slobbers:
'a poem is a city filled with streets and sewers   210
filled with saints, heroes, beggars, madmen,
filled with banality and booze,
filled with rain and thunder and periods of
drought, a poem is a city at war
a poem is a city asking a clock why
a poem is a city burning,
a poem is a city under guns
its barbershops filled with cynical drunks,'

Maneos composes:
'a poem is a garden filled with carnations and poppies
filled with pearl-pale vales
filled with bloomfall fallen from the Arabian moon
filled with intense passion and tense kisses
filled with moments of momentous lust
filled with glens dripping of stars and solitude
a poem is a palace of wheat thirsting for dew-bursts
a poem is a palace peopled with crystalline crystals
a poem is a palace flowing with blood and song.
Its libraries aflurry with Romantic artists.'

Bukowski slobbers:
' my uncle Jack   211

is a mouse
is a house on fire
is a war about to begin
is a man running down the street with a knife in his back.

my uncle Jack
is the Santa Monica pier
is a dusty blue pillow
is a scratching black-and-white dog
is a man with one arm lighting a cigarette with one hand.

my uncle Jack
is a slice of burnt toast
is the place you forgot to look for the key
is the pleasure of finding 3 rolls of toilet paper in the closet
is the worst dream you've ever had that you can't remember.

my uncle Jack
is the firecracker that went off in your hand
is your run-over cat dead outside your driveway at 10:30 a.m.
is the crap game you won in the Santa Anita parking lot
is the man your woman left you for that night in the cheap hotel
room.

my uncle Jack
is your uncle Jack
is death coming like a freight train
is a clown with weeping eyes
is your car jack and your fingernails and the scream of the biggest
mountain now.'

Maneos composes:
' My lover
is a fountain of jasmine sent from sweetly-scented mountains
is a bushel of golden corolla
is a surreal splash of sunset
is a phantasma of gardenia.

My lover
is a leisurely walk in a Florentine garden
is a coronet of dancing moonbeams

is a dream of dripping euphoria
is a tussock of Tuscan night-song.

My lover
is an onslaught of haughty diamonds
is an orgiastic rush of orgasmic ecstasy
is a dale of light-dappled nightingales
is a poetic frenzy of frenzied poetry.

My lover
is a violent kiss of violet-rain
is a whisper of starry-eyed starlings
is a wisp of winking beryl
is a diffuse sentence sentenced to literary immortality.'

XVII

Bukowski slobbers:
'Chinaski, she says, you think you   212
write great stuff but it's all only
a pisspot full of dirty
words!'

Maneos composes:
'Pietros, she says, you think you
write Immortal Poems, but it's all
only a laundry list of pretty words!'

Bukowski slobbers:
'it's so easy to slide into   213
poetic pretension.

almost all art is shot through with
poetic
pretension:'

Maneos composes:
'it's so easy to slide into
Modern minimalism.

Almost all of Modern Poetry is rife
with Modern minimalism.'

Bukowski slobbers:
'there is a letter from a girl   214
at Vassar
at my elbow.
she writes that she is
doing a paper on me:
"Vulgar Literature."

Maneos composes:
'there is a letter from a girl
attending the American University in Rome.
She writes that she is doing a paper on me:
Aesthetic Poetry.'

Bukowski slobbers:
'I'm proud, however, that   215
my work is considered to be
"Vulgar Literature"
by some lady at Vassar!'

Maneos composes:
'I'm proud, however, that
already two of my literary
heroes have praised my
'Aesthetic Sensibility."

Bukowski slobbers:
'what I liked about e.e. cummings   216
was that he cut away from
the holiness of the
word'

Maneos composes:
'What I liked about Helprin
was that he treated *The Word*
as if it was a sacrosanct entity.
A prose filled with more roses

than the whole of Modern Poetry.'

Bukowski slobbers:
'she liked e.e. cummings, though,
she thought he was really
good and she was
right.'

Maneos composes:
'He loved Hila Sedighi, though.
He thought she was a Romantic Revolutionary,
and he was right:
A trinity of tremendous Beauty –
Her Poetry
Her Body
And her Psyche.

He would lose himself in a dazzling daze for days on end
listening to nothing … nothing … save her pleasing singing.
Her tongue, of honey and fire
Rich with flowers and lava –
The very definition of Passion!

Seeing her recite her mighty poesy
with the resounding fury of a furious volcano –
A volcano spewing stars, songs and carnations,
A volcano smitten with the smoldering embers of lightning,
A volcano fired with sun-fire, moon-fire, and sapphires,
Made him feel like Alexander before Roxanne,
most beautiful of the Persians.

On the mythical rocks of Sodgia
Amidst the fallen heroes of proud Bactria
Overcome with Emotion and Longing,
he swore to loud-thundering Zeus, on High:

if Ali Khamenei wounds
a single hair on her Holy Body
I will personally avenge her Sufferings with raging ferocity –

Letting the dogs, the hyenas, and the vultures defile his vile corpse!'

Bukowski slobbers:
'and when I hung up I was sure I could hear 218
Pound, Jeffers, Auden, and Lawrence
laughing in the
dark.'

Maneos composes:
'And when she left, I was sure I could hear
Swinburne, Caravaggio, Neruda and even
Dionysus himself – dancing, clapping and shouting.'

Bukowski slobbers:
'if I have any advice about writing 219
poetry, it's-
don't. I'm going to send out for
some fried chicken.

          buk'

Maneos composes:
'If I have any advice about writing
poetry, it's
travel. Tomorrow I'm leaving for Mytilene
to visit Alcaeus and Sappho.

-Pietros, lover of the lyre,'

Bukowski slobbers:
'the boys 220
are playing the poetry game
again
putting down
meaningless lines
and
passing them off as art
again.'

Maneos composes:

'Chinaski
is playing the literary game
again
publishing horrid poems
and
horrendous novels.
Yet, the unconscious cognoscenti
who have no sense of Beauty
are crowning him with laurels.'

Bukowski slobbers:
'I stand in the kitchen
halfway to madness
dreaming of Hemingway's
Spain.'

221

Maneos composes:
'I stand in the gymnasium
halfway to madness
dreaming of a Roman ludus.'

Bukowski slobbers:
'Hemingway I read everywhere,
sometimes a few times over
and he made me feel brave
and tough'

222

Maneos composes:
'Homer I read everywhere,
sometimes I'll read a single line several times –
pining for a forgotten Time.'

Bukowski slobbers:
'downstairs
I have a large photo of Hemingway
drunk before noon in Havana, he's on the floor
mouth open, his big belly trying to flop
out of his shirt.'

223

Maneos composes:

'downstairs
I have a large photo of dashing D'Annunzio
posing at the Capponcina with a rose tucked within his flashy coat.
He is dandified and defiant as usual.'

Bukowski slobbers:
'I don't know where I read   224
T.S. Eliot.
he made a small dent
which soon ironed
out.'

Maneos composes:
'Sitting in Bacchus' Temple in
Ravello's *Villa Cimbrone*, I began to
satirize canonized Eliot.'

Bukowski slobbers:
'I dropped the magazine to the   225
floor, got up, walked to the
bathroom
and had one of my best
bowel movements in
several years.'

Maneos composes:
'I gently placed Pindar on the floor,
grabbed my strigil,
and walked into the gymnasia,
where I had one of my best workouts in several years.'

XVIII

Bukowski slobbers:
'I disliked the poetic prose   226
right off.
I put the book down and
looked about the
room.'

Maneos composes:
'I fell in love with the poetic prose of Vernon Lee.
I didn't put her book down for two days.'

Bukowski slobbers:
'the users
of exotic words
have discouraged me
from trying to use my
vocabulary
as if it was
a shield
for pretenders.'

227

Maneos composes:
'I have always been attracted
to exotic musical words, with perhaps
my favorite being
tintinnabulation.'

Bukowski slobbers:
'sometimes it seems that only the disabled
and insane like to read my books,
the ones who can't quite grasp
Chaucer.'

228

Maneos composes:
'sometimes it seems that only the
Italians, the Greeks, and the Latins
appreciate my poetry, cultures
that ardently adore Intense Emotion.'

Bukowski slobbers:
'I had been up until 3 a.m. the night before.
heavy drinking: beer, vodka, wine
and there I was at the track
on a Sunday.'

229

Maneos composes:
'I had been up until 3 a.m. the night before –

listening to the wistful lyre from Crete, writing misty-eyed poetry.'

Bukowski slobbers:
'this one teaches   230
and that one lives with his mother
and that one is writing the story of
Ezra Pound.'

Maneos composes:
'this one is a run-away from Andalusia,
That one is descended from The Wild One, Theodoros Kolokotronis.
And she is writing the story of glorious, Odysseas Androutsos.'

Bukowski slobbers:
'but right now   231
it's Bob Dylan
Bob Dylan Bob
Dylan all the
way.'

Maneos composes:
'but right now
it's Achilleas Dramountanis,
Achilleas Dramountanis all the way.
A true Dionysus!'

Bukowski slobbers:
'and listening to   232
Wagner.'

Maneos composes:
'And worshipping the Genius
of Verdi!'

Bukowski slobbers:
'Wagner was a roaring miracle   233
of dark energy.'

Maneos composes:
'Mascagni was a blessing

of beautiful singing.'

Bukowski slobbers:
'and when his draft beers
really got to him
he'd get up and play
Bonaparte's Retreat
6 or 7 times
running.'
234

Maneos composes:
'As I write this, I am listening
to Cheb Khaled's *Liberte*.
Rai is truly the crown-jewel of Bedouin Poetry.

And I am grateful to the great Sting
for introducing the soulful singing
of Cheb Mami
to the rest of Society.'

Bukowski slobbers:
'these dark nights
I begin to feel like
the Chinese poet
Li Po:
drinking wine and writing
poems
writing poems and drinking
wine
235

all the while
aware of the strict limitations
that come with
being
human'

Maneos composes:
'During these crazed nights
I begin to feel like
the Greek poet

Archilochos:
Training in the gymnasium and writing
poems
Writing poems and training in the
gymnasium.

All the while transcending the limitations of humanity.'

Bukowski slobbers:
'I weep like Li Po   236
laugh like Artaud
write like Chinaski.'

Maneos composes:
'I weep like Odysseus
laugh like Juvenal
sing like Orpheus.'

Bukowski slobbers:
'when you write a poem it   237
needn't be intense'

Maneos composes:
'I am closer to blood, to lava, than to ink.'

Bukowski slobbers:
'I had to take a shit   238
but instead I went
into this shop to
have a key made.'

Maneos composes:
'I had to train my arms
for tomorrow's photo-shoot,
but instead I went into the library
to read Nonnus.'

XIX

Bukowski slobbers:
'I used to like Monet   239
I used to like Monet very much
it was funny, I thought, the way he did it
with colors'

Maneos composes:
'I've always hated Basquiat
I've always hated Basquiat with a searing passion.
It was barbaric, I thought, what he did with stick-figures:
Surely, Samo is no Michelangelo.'

Bukowski slobbers:
"where were you," I   240
asked her," when I was living
on one candy bar a day and
sending short stories to the
Atlantic Monthly?"

Maneos composes:
'Where were you,' I
asked her, 'when I was living
on canned tuna, and
writing love-pained poems
on stained napkins?'

Bukowski slobbers:
'I promised I would write an essay ON THE MEANING   241
    OF
MODERN POETRY'

Maneos composes:
'I promised her that I would write an acerbic poem attacking Modern
Poetry,
while defending 'To Eu' and 'To Kalon."

Bukowski slobbers:
'what am I doing alone   242
drunk and writing poems at
3:18 a.m.?'

Maneos composes:
'What am I doing composing poetry
in the midst of this mythic Beauty?'

XX

Bukowski slobbers:
'my present editor-publisher   243
and I
at times
did discuss the thirties,
the Depression
and
some of the little tricks it
taught us-'

Maneos composes:
'my present publisher
and I are feuding, but that doesn't
stop us from discussing the Greek mind,
the most recent Archaeological finds,
and the Immortal Poetic Lines
that the Ancients left behind.'

Bukowski slobbers:
'eating out tonight   244
I find a table alone
and while waiting for my order
take out my wife's copy of
A Poet in New York.
I often carry things to read
so that I will not have to look at
the people.

I find the poems bad (for me)'

Maneos composes:
'Eating sushi tonight under the swooning moonlight
I find a table – alone –

While waiting for my order
I take out my copy of
LOVE IS A DOG FROM HELL

I find the poems vulgar, prosaic, and vapid (for me),
so I replace it with Lorca's *A POET IN NEW YORK*.'

Bukowski slobbers:
'he likes rugged stuff   245
where I write across the painting ---
"shoot shit" or "GRATE ART IS
HORSESHIT, BUY TACOS."

Maneos composes:
'She adores fervent poetry
So I write across the blood-stained parchment:
Szerelem szerelem   246
Atkozott szerelem
Szerelem szerelem
Atkozott szerelm'

Bukowski slobbers:
'yes, poetry is a lie.'   247

Maneos composes:
'Yes, Poetry is Olympian.'

Bukowski slobbers:
'it   248
takes
a lot of

desperation

dissatisfaction

and
disillusion

to

write

a
few
good
poems.'

Maneos composes:
It takes a lot of Passion,
Emotion,
and Ecstasy,
to compose rosy-souled poesy.

And to bring forth Beauty
from one's personal sufferings
is certainly holy.'

Bukowski slobbers:
'poetry is what happens   249
when nothing else
can.'

Maneos composes:
'Poetry is the insistent roaring of the human soul.'

XXI

I had planned to write numerous blurbs on the barbarous bard, Allen
Ginsberg
But then, on advice from a friend,
I decided to defend The Beautiful
in one single comic vignette.
So here goes my descent into irony
and full blown mockery.

Ginsberg scrawls:
'America I've given you all and now I'm nothing.   250
America two dollars and twentyseven cents January 17, 1956.
I can't stand my own mind.
America when will we end the human war?
Go fuck yourself with your atom bomb.
I don't feel good don't bother me.
I won't write my poem till I'm in my right mind.
America when will you be angelic?
When will you take off your clothes?
When will you look at yourself through the grave?
When will you be worthy of your million Trotskyites?
America why are your libraries full of tears?
America when will you send your eggs to India?'

Maneos chuckles:
'America, I've given you nothing and now I'm nothing.
How could this be?
America, why are you still reading me?
America 1 dolla, 2 lire and 32 shekels
March 24th, 2009.
What horrible poverty!

When will you realize that I'm a bad poet?
America, when will you understand that me and my beaten friends are
mediocre?
(Is that the proper grammar? shouldn't it be 'my beaten friends and I?'
Get me a fucking grammarian!)

America – you're such a pompous ogre.
Wait, who is America?
I'm America. Maybe I'm not.
Maybe I'm Chinese or Russian.
Yes, in a past life, I was a Chinese Prussian whose mother was
Russian,
Or was it Tuscan?
I can't remember. Anyways.

When will I be given free handouts? I love handouts.
I demand free food, free housing, and free sex!
Don't you hate having to pay for sex?
Or having to wait for food?

When will the 3 Trotskyites take over America?
Oh wait, Marxism is dead.
Except in the ivory towers of the Ivy League.
He's a super duper star there.

America, I smoke crack every chance I get.
Maybe this is why my poetry is god-awful.
America, I sit in my closet staring at my television set.

America, I'm not a lawful citizen.
I'm the enemy within. I'm Sean Hannity's nightmare.
He's such a repressive square.

America, I don't support the NRA.
But I think all capitalists should be shot!
America, if I shaved my beard, I'd be so hot.
America, Mumia Abu Jamal must not die: even if he killed a cop

America – I worship the ugly and shun The Beautiful.
(All profoundly original art looks ugly at first, right?
Isn't that the party-line now?)
Look at how we savaged, Tom Wolfe!
That conservative! That philistine!!!

Have you hugged a tree today or saved a whale? I have.
Are you proud of me?

America, I'll have you know that I'm a Buddhist, a Hinduist and a Communist.
Wait, is that possible? Hey Jack, come over here for a second – 'Is Hinduist a word?'

America when will you send your children to fight in Bahrain??
'No more blood for oil! No more blood for oil'
America my psychoanalyst thinks I'm certifiably insane.

Jesus Christ, I smell of urine!
Can someone hose me off?

America I have reopened the whorehouses in Tangiers.
Sometimes, I dress as a woman, and play the part of the Madam
I have done this for no less than five years!

America when I was young my mother took me to a daisy store and you should have seen the beauty, but your pollution killed all of the daises.
Now, there are no more daisies for me to smell.
I demand more daisies!!!!
Yes, I demand more daisies! More daisies! More daisies!
America, I just realized that I'm a babbling fool.
Ssssh. Don't tell anyone.

I'm now addressing two homeless ducks.
BRAINS MAN!

I hate American culture!
I just realized that I am American culture.
Wait, does this mean that I hate myself?
Great! An existential dilemma! Get Sartre on the phone now!!!!

(In my past life, I was a strict formalist)
Ssssh. Please don't tell Kerouac or Gioia
They might be pissed.

America you better consider your natural resources!
My resources consist of reams of bad poetry, dreams of vile barbarity, and streams of unutterable vulgarity.

My ambition is to be mayor of Berkeley, despite the fact that I am
losing my hair.
America, I have homosexual visions and cosmic vibrators.
Does that frighten you?

I love barbarism!
I am the Great Barbarian!
Hear me roar!
I am the National Bard of the Visigoths,
And the poet laureate of the Alemani.
I mean, the Americans.

Who is Mr. Norton?
And why is my poetry in his anthology?

America, I'm obsessed with Hustler Magazine.
I read it every chance I get.
I bet that makes you upset.
America, I hate your heroes.
You know what, I hate all heroes.
I celebrate losers.
I'm a loser and a boozer.
'I'm a loser baby, so why don't you kill me.'   251

I'm the hero (Or is it the anti-hero) of the EMO crowd and the New
York hipsters!
They think I'm so rebellious and soooooooooo counter-culture.
But wait, isn't the counter-culture now the dominant culture,
so am I now counter-counter-culture?
I'm so confused!

I wish I lived in Seattle.
It rains there though, but at least it doesn't snow. Or does it?
Hey, get me a weatherman over here.
I need to know the climate in Seattle.
Goddamnit, does it snow in Seattle or not!?!?

But if I move, I'll probably miss San Francisco:
Haight-Ashbury is home to the worst poets known.

We battle over whose writing is the ugliest, I mean, the most
INNOVATIVE!
Make it new! Make it new! Make it new!

America, when will you allow the Chinese or the Russians to conquer
you?
I think it's time you fell.
Don't you?
You oughta burn all of your F-22s!
Then, make peace with the Persians, errr, I mean Iranians, and the
Chinese!!!!
The Dong-Feng 21D is a missile of peace, right???????
America, don't be blue.

It's your own foreign policy that caused this catastrophic mess.
You're such a beastly imperialist.
At least that's what Chomsky and Sontag tell us.

Obama's execution of Osama was unjust
And something out of the Wild West
What kind of terrorists shoot an unarmed man?

America – I am your greatest logician,
And your greatest magician!

Down with American imperialism!
Death to all capitalists!!! Death to all capitalists!!!
America, I have no concept of *aisthetics*.
Wait, did I even spell that right?
Hold on, let me get a dictionary.

America – James Franco thinks I'm a Genius!
So there! Take that!

The Emperor has no clothes! The Emperor has no clothes! The
Emperor has no clothes!'

XXII

Prosaic O'Hara is not able to create a verbal mosaic.
This does not surprise me,
For he was schooled by the ghoulish New York School:
A minimalist movement littered with mediocre fools, vulgar ogres and
barbaric rules:
A veritable cesspool of dripping gruel.

O'Hara drips:
'where is Gary Snyder I wonder if he's reading under a dwarf pine   252
stretched out so his book and his head fit under the lowest branch
while the sun of the Orient rolls calmly not getting through to him'

Maneos sculpts:
'Where is Frances Mayes?
I wonder if she's dining in France,
Tasting wine in Chiusi,
Or having a laugh in Sicily?

What a glorious soul – a student of Passion!
A bard, a gardener, an ardent cultivator of liquid gold –
Whose spirit yearns for the golden Italian-Sun
Just like the Etruscans of old.

A beautiful anomaly in culture –
For her whole life has been a love-letter
to Tuscany, to Italy,
to the very idea of Beauty.'

O'Hara drips:
'Where is Mike Goldberg? I don't know,   253
he may be in the Village far below
or lounging on Tenth Street with the gang
of early-morning painters (before noon)
as they discuss the geste or jest
of action painting,'

Maneos sculpts:
'Where is Ferenc Mate, that Maestro

of Brunello?
Is he sailing into an Italian Bay,
Dancing in a Tuscan winery,
Or composing prose as poetic as any poetry?'

O'Hara drips:
'where's Lana Turner   254
she's out eating
and Garbo's backstage at the Met
everyone's taking their coat off
so they can show a rib-cage to the rib-watchers'

Maneos sculpts:
"Where's Tebaldi?'
'She's eating her heart out on the outskirts of La Scala
listening to the brazen shouts praising the sweet singing of Callas.
Yet everyone admits that Renata
should have been the first choice,
For hers is the superior voice."

O'Hara drips:
'Miss Lombard, this is a young   255
movie actor who just died
in his Porsche Spyder sportscar
near Paso Robles on his way
to Salinas for a race. This is
James Dean, Carole Lombard. I hope
you will be good to him up there.'

Maneos sculpts:
'The Dying Gladiator, a Syrian Secutor, with blood and sand upon his
brow
Knows now that the slow death-blow
is close at hand.
For here in the Primus,
surrounded by the Roman demos,
clemency is given to no man.
Yet, despite this,
he faces his Fate like the famous Hero, Patroclus:
With nigh a grimace, seething contemptuous Defiance!'

O'Hara drips:
James Dean
actor
made in USA
eager to be everything
stopped short

Do we know what
excellence is? it's
all in this world
not to be executed'

Maneos sculpts:
Oh Diakos!
How I wish I was with you in Roumeli!
Fighting next to the blossoming cypress tree
Bleeding profusely,
so that one day Greece may be free!

Oh, Olympian Divinities!
Please, let me be one of the great 48!
Destined for a truly heroic Fate!
Defending Liberty against Tyranny,
while fulfilling a Homeric Destiny!

Oh Diakos!
Let us resist the invidious invaders
like our ancestors of yesteryear
who fought like Lions, devoid of any fear –
Like Spartans clashing with The Barbarians!
Protecting these hallowed lands
from the clutches of Persian hands.
Like the Cretans against the Germans,
Or like a klepht or a brave palikari,
slaying the mighty Ottomans!

Oh Diakos!
I wish to garland you in sprigs of spring-basil
Bushels of laurel

And wreathes of fennel!
Honoring your glorious story with my sword of swinging fire,
My wondrous words soaring into Pierian wings,
and the starry singing of my glistening lyre.

Oh Diakos!
I wish to bleed on the very spot where you so gloriously fell!
Where the blood of high-hearted Heroes
water these breezy meadows –
Planting indomitable boughs – boughs of Freedom!
Look at the time Charon chose to take me
Now that the branches are flowering
And the earth sends forth grass.

Oh Diakos!
You are the equal of Immortal Leonidas,
The very spirit of Hellas!
But where does your bold soul now sleep?
Are you with Androutsos in Gravia?
Or in Missolonghi with Nikitaras?
Yet some say that you weep
upon the slavish streets of Nicosia –
Dreaming of the colossal battle of Alamana –
Hoping for just one more last stand,
fighting to the very last man!

Oh Diakos, I wish to die with you once again,
my fearless friend,
even if it's just the two of us
versus the best of men
from Northern Cyprus!'

O'Hara drips:
'O the dark!
I the TV!
O the various marvelous lotions each costing $12 per ounce of plankton!'

Maneos sculpts:
'Oh Solomos Solomou!
We have not forgotten you –

For you have taught us the value
of manly virtue.
And someday soon, phile mou,
We shall avenge you!'

O'Hara drips:
'didn't you know we was all going to be Zen Buddhists after   258
what we did you sure don't know much about war-guilt
or nothin and the peach trees continued to rejoice around
the prick which was for once authorized by our Congress
though inactive what if it had turned out to be a volcano'

Maneos sculpts:
'To those who love Freedom
Be it from the Cross, the Crescent
or any form of oppressive Government –
Wield your sword and shield
in these daisy-filled fields.
Yield not a foot – take not a step back
Leave this world with every wound on your front
And nary a scratch on your back!'

XXIII

O'Hara drips:
'There are several Puerto   259
Ricans on the avenue today, which
makes it beautiful and warm. First
Bunny died, then John Latouche,
then Jackson Pollock'

Maneos sculpts:
'There are several Florentine painters descended from the master –
Giovanni Bellini – passing through Rome today.
They are nibbling cannelloni on Via Barberini while quibbling over
the merits of Guido Reni.
(By the way, is Pollock still hawking his bestial 'action' paintings?)'

O'Hara drips:
'Maude lays down her doll, red wagon and her turtle   260

takes my hand and comes with us, shows the bronze JACKSON POLLOCK
gazelling on the rock of her demeanor as a child, says running
away hand in hand "he isn't under there, he's out in the woods" beyond'

Maneos sculpts:
'Francesca led us down the hall of the Bargello
to show us the bronze David by DONATELLO
A masterpiece in its own right,
Yet I still prefer Bernini's to DONATELLO'S
For it has a touch of Alexander's divine might.'

O'Hara drips:
'in the middle of a rather tendentious movie on Kant   261
dreams of chocolate-cream pie are a relief'

Maneos sculpts:
'in the middle of a rather well-done film on Pollock
dreams of an Aesthetic Revolution stream into my mind!'

O'Hara drips:
'just as at home I never think of the *Nude Descending a Staircase* or   262
at a rehearsal a single drawing of Leonardo or Michelangelo that used to
wow me'

Maneos sculpts:
'Just as in my atelier, I paint over the mustache and goatee in
Duchamp's *Mona Lisa*
before pissing in his *Fountain*.'

O'Hara drips:
'Why must all Russian composers   try to be brave'   263

Maneos sculpts:
'Why is most Modernist Poetry devoid of Beauty?'

O'Hara drips:
'   the acrid dryness of your paper   264
already reminded of
                  New York's sky in August before the

---

nasal rains'

Maneos sculpts:
'the Baroque lushness of your play
reminded me of a decadent day
before a floral festival in blissful Pompeii.'

O'Hara drips:
'   I sit with Ashbery 265
in the Flore because of his poem about himself in a flower-bed
and we look for Gregory in the Deux Magots because I want to cry with
him
about a dear dead friend, it's always about dying, never about death'

Maneos sculpts:
'I sit with Gabriela Dellosso
in the loggia –
worshipping the Poet-Hero,
Gabriele,
relaying his love of *Arete*
and his fleshy forays into far-fabled Pompeii.'

O'Hara drips:
'   I first recognized art   266
as wildness, and it seemed right,
                    I mean rite, to me'

Maneos sculpts:
'I first recognized Art
as the pursuit of Beauty, so it seemed right
for me to worship the fleeting moon-light.'

O'Hara drips:
'O Willem de Kooning, you are a very great man   267
for saying what you said about him and I love you.'

Maneos sculpts:
'O Willem de Kooning, you are a vile villain
for bungling art, and I hate you!:
'In every Raphael there are a hundred million de Koonings.   268

In de Kooning there is not a single Raphael."

O'Hara drips:
'Well, I have my beautiful de Kooning   269
to aspire to. I think it has an orange
bed in it, more than the ear can hold.'

Maneos sculpts:
'Well, I have my stunning Tomasz Rut
to aspire to. Yet, I would give vials of blood to see Polyclitus'
Canon.'

O'Hara drips:
'   He thinks with pleasure that   270
his first name is the same as de Kooning's.
People even call him "Bill" too, and
they often smile.'

Maneos sculpts:
'Oh for Sabah Fakhri,
and the lutes and flutes of Syria!
As the ecstasies of Arabian Poetry
comingle with the lyras of Tunisia
I am completely conquered
by the joyous voice
of muse-blessed Fakhri:
A devotee of eternal, ethereal Beauty.
A child of Hafiz, Rumi,
and the wild-whirling Sufis.

Aman! Aman! Come dance with me, my heroic friend.
Let us spend the evening given to Dionysian dancing:
Twirling madly to the violin
as its hypnotic sounds
resound like a Spartan paean
or an Athenian hymn
enveloping the holy plains of Marathon;
extolling the virtues of Grecian Freedom.'

O'Hara drips:

'I have another cognac
and stare at two little paintings
of Jean-Paul's, so great
I must do so much
or did they just happen'

Maneos sculpts:
'I have another glass of vino
and stare at two monumental paintings
of Rut's – so beautiful and full of pathos.'

O'Hara drips:
'   I am so glad that Larry Rivers made a
statue of me

        and now I hear that my penis is on all
the statues of all the young sculptors who've
seen it'

Maneos sculpts:
'I am elated that Tomasz Rut painted me
in the idealized Grecian manner –
As if I were some far-flung Hero from Homer,
Or a wreathed athlete
sprung from the pages of Pindar
capable of performing Olympian feats.'

O'Hara drips:
'Sitting in a corner of the gallery
I notice that Albers scratches a tiny A
in the lower right corner with the date
and the paintings are like floodlights
on my emptiness'

Maneos sculpts:
'Gazing at Caravaggio's *The Musicians*
I am reminded that nothing can move
the soul quite like a tragic song.
There is tremendous Beauty
found in profound melancholy.'

O'Hara drips:
'he had an autocratic straw face like a dark   274
in a de Kooning where the torrent has subsided at the very center
of classicism,'

Maneos sculpts:
'He had a heroic demeanor like the Byron of Thorvaldsen
where the love of Classicism meets the far-off gaze of Romanticism.'

O'Hara drips:
'Oh, I forgot to excerpt something else, a little description of   275
a de Kooning WOMAN
which I'd seen recently at his studio:

>You remained for me a green Buick of sighs, o Gladstone!
>and your wife Trina, how like a yellow pillow on a sill
>in the many-windowed dusk where the air is compartmented!
>her red lips of Hollywood, soft as a Titian and as tender,
>her gray face which refrains from thrusting aside the mane
>of your languorous black smells, the hand crushed by her chin,
>and that slumberland of dark cutaneous lines which reels
>under the burden of her many-darkly-hued corpulence of linen
>and satin bushes, is like a lone rose with the sky behind it.
>A yellow rose. Valentine's Day . . .'

Maneos sculpts:
'Oh, I forgot to show you something else, a little poem about Neda
Soltan, who was martyred by the animals of the Iranian Basij during
The Revolution in 2009:

Men will say, why doesn't your poetry speak of Love?
Of poppies singing with the petals of poplars
Of tulips dripping from your lips
Of burnished amethyst kissing the cousins-of-pearls?
Where are the young girls dancing in Sapphic circles?

Where are the gemstones caressed by gleaming moonbeams?
What of the Homeric heroes that fight mightily
between the dreamy lines of your poesy?

Why does your lyre lie silent, dormant as a placid monk?

I will tell you – come and see the blood in Tehran!
Come and see the blood in the streets!
Come and see the lifeless body of Neda Soltan!

Oh Neda – lover of The Beautiful
Student of the Muses, daughter of Euterpe –
Graceful, Beautiful, Immortal!

Oh Neda Soltan!
Your violent death rivals the valiant Athenians at Marathon,
For like them, you stood for Freedom against Tyranny –
You died heroically: brave, proud and most importantly, Free!

Oh Neda – I salute you.
For you gave the highest sacrifice one can give – your very Life!
I send you blue-flowers stolen from the flower-tipped tips of Olympus
I send you blood from my vivacious verse:
Lines lined with fine wines, ambrosial linens, and fragrant incense.

I mourn your senseless demise,
And I curse the accursed Basij;
I condemn the ranting tyrants who have besieged the soul of your
country –
Enslaving its people under the fanaticism of fanatical religiosity.
Murderers, Puppeteers, Animals!
Propagandists of Despair! Slave-Masters of the Soul!

So today, my friend, I send you my humble kisses,
Blessed by the music of the muses:
The sounds of the resounding lyra
And arias steeped in the blood of wisteria.

Truly, a hero's song that burns only for you, my Neda.'

XXIV

O'Hara drips:
'Picasso made me tough and quick, and the world;'   276

112

Maneos sculpts:
'Rossetti made me aesthetic and poetic.'

O'Hara drips:
'it is a great period of Italian art when everyone imitates Picasso   277
afraid to mean anything'

Maneos sculpts:
'it is a great period of Italian art when everyone is inspired by the
ancient Hellenes:
Inimitable in its depiction of *The Beautiful*.'

O'Hara drips:
'   Clement Greenberg the discoverer,   278
Harold Rosenberg the analyzer, and so on and so on.

Maneos sculpts:
'Zeuxis the progenitor, Winckelmann the disciple, and Tomasz Rut the
glorious philhellene.'

O'Hara drips:
"New York is everywhere like Paris!'   279

Maneos sculpts:
'The New York art scene is filled with mindless philistines,
Slaves to the concept of the *avant-fraud*
Blindly leaping from one trend to the next.'

O'Hara drips:
'no we love us still hanging   280
around the paintings Richard Burton
waves through de Kooning the
Wild West rides up out of the Pollock'

Maneos sculpts:
'we love dancing in the Arcadian fields of Edward Schmidt,
discussing the marvelous paintings of Jacob Collins,
and losing ourselves in the forgotten worlds,
emerging from the Water Street Atelier:

a lone ray of light amidst so much Modernist darkness!'

O'Hara drips:
'There is the Pollock, white, harm   281
will not fall, his perfect hand'

Maneos sculpts:
'There are the Giotto frescoes in Assisi
and the tale of his perfect circle relayed by Vasari'

O'Hara drips:
'A fine day for seeing. I see   282
ceramics, during lunch hour, by
Mir6, and I see the sea by Leger;
light, complicated Metzingers
and a rude awakening by Brauner,
a little table by Picasso, pink.'

Maneos sculpts:
'A fine day for seeing.
During my lunch-hour,
I see amphorae by Lydos, paintings by Panini
and sculptures by Bernini.
Then, with a few friends, I see the trembling sea with my own eyes:
Waves dancing below
the iridescent light liquefied by the incandescent skies.'

O'Hara drips:
'Are you effeminate, like an eyelid, or are you feminine,   283
like a painting by Picasso?'

Maneos sculpts:
'Are you lifeless, like an Imagist, or impassioned
like a painting by Delacroix?'

O'Hara drips:
'Have you been to Mike Goldberg's show? Al Leslie's?   284
 Lee Krasner's?'

Maneos sculpts:

'Have you been to Gabriela Dellosso's show? Michael Newberry's?
Sabin Howard's?
Bravo!

Despite the intent of Modernist Artists and Theorists to diminish *To
Kallos*
It persists like Ovidian kisses hiding in the mists of Tomis,
Like sea-foam foaming in sea-born Paphos,
And like the Sapphic lyre singing on the cloven cliffs of fiery Lesbos.'

O'Hara drips:
'   Guernica hollered look out!   285
but we were all busy hoping our eyes were talking
to Paul Klee. My mother and father asked me and
I told them from my tight blue pants we should
love only the stones, the sea, and heroic figures.
Wasted child! I'll club you on the shins! I
wasn't surprised when the older people entered
my cheap hotel room and broke my guitar and my can
of blue paint.'

Maneos sculpts:
'Graydon Parrish's *Victory* personifies Pure Beauty.
The billowing garland,
flowing into the winged wind,
is surely a gift from Arcadian gardens,
the lovely land of lively Pan.

The body carefully contoured and nigh Olympian.
The flesh as if crafted from pure Parian,
And the profile chiseled from the stolen one, far-renowned Helen.

An epic poem could be composed solely upon the slight
dimple in her lower back:
A rivulet resplendent with honied light
A chalice rich with amber and ambrosia,
And a flowering ravine ravished with the dreamy flowers of Roma!

How could one not worship such divine loveliness?
Truly, she is a goddess fallen from hallowed Olympus!'

O'Hara drips:
'   so I get back up   286
make coffee, and read Francois Villon, his life, so dark
     New York seems blinding and my tie is blowing up the street
I wish it would blow off'

Maneos sculpts:
'so I get back up
to make a cup of espresso,
before reading Caesar's *The Conquest of Gaul*.
How glorious!
Rome seems a comfort to those with the ambitious soul of an Artist or
a Conqueror.'

O'Hara drips:
'   I wrap myself in the robes of your whiteness which is   287
like mid-night in Dostoevsky.'

Maneos sculpts:
'I wrap myself in the robes of your ardent love which is like a
sun-speared sunset in Lermontov.'

O'Hara drips:
'   So you do not like   288
my new verses, written in the
pages of Russian novels while I do
not brood over an orderly
childhood?'

Maneos sculpts:
'So you do not like
my new verses, written in the
pages of Sapphic fragments in
between dreams of Hellenic conquest?'

O'Hara drips:
'why do I always read   289
Russian exile novels in
summer I guess because

they're full of snow'

Maneos sculpts:
'Why do I always read Hellenic poetry in the Winter -
I guess because the world is so vulgar,
And these very poems define The Beautiful.'

O'Hara drips:
'
                            Ionesco is greater   290
than Beckett, Vincent said,'

Maneos sculpts:
"Ionesco is as abysmal, as vile, and as absurd
as Beckett,' Roberto said,'

O'Hara drips:
'O Kenneth Koch!'   291

Maneos sculpts:
'O sweet-smiling, sweet-singing Sappho!'

O'Hara drips:
'I'm getting rather Lorcaesque lately   292
and I don't like it.'

Maneos sculpts:
'I'm getting rather Lorca-esque lately and I like it.
For this very evening, I've fallen in Love with no less than eighteen
shimmering shades of green.'

O'Hara drips:
'I don't know as I get what D.H. Lawrence is driving at   293
when he writes of lust springing from the bowels'

Maneos sculpts:
'I do know what lusty Archilochus is driving at
when he writes of the writhing lust springing from his bowels:

Oh Neobule!
What I would sacrifice to have you on this very day –

For even the mere hint of your shadow sends me
into sudden, shuddering Ecstasies!"

O'Hara drips:
'I reach to the D.H. Lawrence on the floor and read   294
"The Ship of Death"

Maneos sculpts:
'I reach to the D.H. Lawrence on the bed,
which rests upon the soft breast
of my golden-tressed Goddess,
and begin reading 'The Twilight in Italy."

O'Hara drips:
'   They hadn't read   295
Sartre's *Being and Nothingness* for nothing.'

Maneos sculpts:
'They hadn't read Neruda's *Veinte Poemas de amor y una cancion
desesperada* for nothing.'

O'Hara drips:
'it's so   296
original, hydrogenic, anthropomorphic, fiscal, post-anti-esthetic,
          bland, unpicturesque and WilliamCarlosWilliamsian!
it's definitely not 19th century, it's not even Partisan Review, it's
          new, it must be vanguard!'

Maneos sculpts:
'It's so
beautiful, descriptive, pastoral, aurally delicious, aureate, aesthetic,
religious, picturesque and Nerudaean!
It's definitely descended from the 19th century fleshly school,
And if not for the Eliot section, it might be New Criterion.
It's thoroughly Modern, but at the same time Anti-Modern, Romantic
and Classical.'

O'Hara drips:
'Art is sad and   297
life is vapid. Can we thumb

our nose at the very sea?'

Maneos sculpts:
'Art is grand and
life is glorious.
I wish to live forever
amongst these unctuous odalisques'

O'Hara drips:
'I am not interested in good.'   298

Maneos sculpts:
'I am most interested in *The Beautiful*.'

O'Hara drips:
'O my coevals! embarrassing   299
memories! pastiches! jokes!'

Maneos sculpts:
'O Mr. Hallowell, Mistah Kurtz and John Paul!
O Captains!
My Captains!'

O'Hara drips:
'
                               I am the only spy left   300
in Canada,
               but just because I'm alone in the snow
doesn't necessarily mean I'm a Nazi.'

Maneos sculpts:
'I'm one of the few aesthetes
left in the States.
But just because I'm alone,
at the far-famed hot gates,
defending The Beautiful from the Modernist way,
doesn't mean that I'm Joseph Goebbels,
Though maybe Don Quixote.'

XXV

O'Hara drips:
'   CLEMENT GREENBERG
How Orphic?'

CHARLES DICKENS
He hated pretense. He was the founder of Social Security.

LAWRENCE OF ARABIA
Cognac is not KY.

TERESA OF AVILA
My ink is hardly dry upon the page.

SAINT PAUL
The light that failed.

GROVER WHALEN
A hoot he had. A crease he did not. The water crusheth, the booth notth.

PIERRE BOULEZ
In a sense I have not really arrived into your country, yet.

BARON HAUSSMAN
As I see it, everything is at right angles, like the flowers, Kenneth.

ARCHIBALD MACLEISH
I heard a creep swimming by me in the lighthouse.

Maneos sculpts:
'CLEMENT GREENBERG
Barbaros!

ERNEST HEMINGWAY
Yes Ernest, it is pretty to think so.

PURVIS YOUNG
I'm sure that even the Huns, the Vandals, and the Visigoths had painters of some sort.

MARK HELPRIN

A real Aesthete! A real Romantic! My hero!

SAMUEL BECKETT
Godot and I are dancing in an Arcadian nymphaeum with a harem of
nymphs!

JEAN-PAUL SARTRE
I am more interested in this spectacular view from my hotel-room in
Assisi than in his world-view.

MICHAEL NEWBERRY
The William Blake of Idyllwild!

T.E. HULME
'When I sing as I please, I taste blood in my mouth'   302

JONATHAN FRANZEN
The hyper-lyrical is not the faux-literary.

MARCEL DUCHAMP
Che brutto disegno!

CAMILLE PAGLIA
Marry me, La Divina?
I love you, Camille! Even Medea would cower before you!
Viva Paglia!'

O'Hara drips:
'   I hate Vachel Lindsay, always have; I don't even   303
like rhythm, assonance, all that stuff.'

Maneos sculpts:
'So much depends upon
the radiant beauty of the pond.

Flushed with white-roses floating upon
the rose-white water.

And as dawn with her finger-tips of golden-rose
encloses the lips of the horizon,

I swim swiftly
into the reigning rays of the Sun.'

O'Hara drips:
'   The single most important event in his artistic career was   304
when de Kooning said his painting was like pressing your face into wet
grass.'

Maneos sculpts:
'The single greatest compliment that I have ever received was when
Charles Dahl said that reading my novella, *The Italian Pleasures of
Gabriele Paterkallos*, was like flying to Olympus on a winged horse.'

O'Hara drips:
'   The literary establishment   305
cared about as much for our work as the Frick cared for Pollock and de
Kooning, not that we cared any more about establishments than they did,
all of the disinterested parties being honor-able men.'

Maneos sculpts:
'The cultural establishment cared about as much for our style of
literature – 'Il Bel Stil Novo' – 'The Beautiful New Style' – as the
MoMA cared for Classical Realism, though not that Roman Payne or I
really cared about such trifling things as the cultural establishment or
the MoMA.'

O'Hara drips:
'In that sense, the artist's duty to his time has nothing to do with   306
Whether he likes it or not, any more than Picasso liked the idea of the
town of Guernica
being bombed, or the Renaissance painters liked to have Christ crucified
over and over again.'

Maneos sculpts:
'Only one who is either a coward or ahistorical would blindly serve
one's time. In fact, to reject one's time is an artistic statement unto
itself. Thus, what would be more sublime than to sculpt the perfected
torso of the godly hero, Diomedes, adjacent to The Whitney Art
Museum?'

O'Hara drips:
'I am ashamed of my century   307
for being so entertaining
but I have to smile'

Maneos sculpts:
'I am not a man of my century –
which I manifest in both my Homeric Poetry
and my Adonic body.'

XXVI

O'Hara drips:
'Dawn must always recur   308
                        to blot out stars and the terrible systems
of belief'

Maneos sculpts:
'When young dawn undressed her golden tresses just under the
horizon, the wondrous Aegean wept with Joy.'

O'Hara drips:
'Dawn, which dries out the web so the wind can blow it,   309
                        spider and all, away'

Maneos sculpts:
'When young dawn unfurled her golden tassels upon the world, the
harem-girls fell into a spell of whirling Passion.'

O'Hara drips:
'Dawn,   310
            erasing blindness from an eye inflamed,
                                            reaching for its
morning cigarette in Promethean inflection'

Maneos sculpts:
'Dawn, enthroned in gold, enfolded the world in its enchanting
Beauty.'

O'Hara drips:

'Alone at night
in the wet city'

Maneos sculpts:
'The Pleiades burns
I lie alone, spurned.'

O'Hara drips:
'I don't want to fire on the *Pleiades*
        before the iceberg has a chance to sink them

                anything yet, sir? post double lookouts!'

Maneos sculpts:
'Beneath the lonely Pleiades
I listen to the pleas of the whispering breeze,
The pleasing songs of the glistening seas,
And the faint strains of Lesbian strophes.
I realize that the star-dappled skies are the very canvas of the
Divinities.'

O'Hara drips:
'on that particular event on the shore of Asia Minor'

Maneos sculpts:
'On the shapely shores of Asia Minor,
I was floored by Ottoman splendor.'

O'Hara drips:
'*Suddenly that body appears: in my smoke*
while someone's heavily describing Greece,
that famous monotonous line feels white'

Maneos sculpts:
'Just as the isle appeared, the old man smiled
and began intoning:
The isles of Greece! The isles of Greece!'

O'Hara drips:
'I don't have an American   315
body, I have an anonymous body, though
you can get to love it, if you love
the corpses of the Renaissance;'

Maneos sculpts:
'I don't have an American body.
I possess Hellenic symmetria, or rather, symmetry,
descended directly from Polykleitan Beauty.'

O'Hara drips:
'Now what we desire is space.   316
To turn up the thermometer and sigh.'

Maneos sculpts:
'Now what we desire is the honey-voiced lyre
So bring in the dancing women.'

O'Hara drips:
'   Oh space!   317
you never conquer desire, do you?'

Maneos sculpts:
'Oh lyre!
You spark such Homeric desires.'

O'Hara drips:
'I wish to whine all the rest of my life like a kite!'   318

Maneos sculpts:
'I wish to sing all the rest of my life like a lyra!'

O'Hara drips:
'   I'm staying with you   319
fuck Canada'

Maneos sculpts:
'I'm staying here in Izmir for the rest of the year
Fuck the predictable path of my peers.'

O'Hara drips:
'We ate manure
    for lunch
in a house
    in the city.'

Maneos sculpts:
'We ate pastitsio and pastries in Leonidio
before dancing a slow zembekiko
under the sun's hungry glow:
Yasas'

O'Hara drips:
'I am stuck in traffic in a taxicab
which is typical
and not just of modern life'

Maneos sculpts:
'I am stuck in the clutches of my harem-girls, Cyra,
and Delilah,
which is typical of my amoral adventures
in both Susa and Moravia.'

O'Hara drips:
'
                        and you visiting
Cambridge, Massachusetts, talking for two weeks worth
in hours,'

Maneos sculpts:
'and you being able to visit Mytilene, of the lovely dances –
where one dances twenty years worth
in one week of unspeakable revelry.'

O'Hara drips:
'57th Street
street of joy
I am a microcosm in your macrocosm
and then a macrocosm in your miscrocosm
a hydrogen bomb too tiny

to make an eye water
and yet I toddle along
past the reverential windows of Tiffany
with its diamond clips on paper bags'

Maneos sculpts:
'Idling on this idyllic isle,
Olive-rich Lesbos,
while composing rosy pastorals and commanding idylls
with the assistance of Orpheus and Musaeus.
Roving through the olive groves,
the rolling hills filled with the trilling of muse-loving timbrels,
while singing the living hymns of Theocritus.
This – this existence is a slice of Paradise,
a small sliver of the mysterious afterlife.'

O'Hara drips:
'I have another cognac   324
and stare at two little paintings
of Jean-Paul's, so great
I must do so much
or did they just happen'

Maneos sculpts:
'I have another ouzo with a famed balladeer from Izmir,
Before reading fragments of torrid Anacreon –
so great that I feel inferior.'

O'Hara drips:
'   my asiatic tendencies have taken me   325
to the Baghdad of neurasthenia and
false objectivity'

Maneos sculpts:
'My Asiatic tendencies cause me
to shout 'Ore'
in the midst of miming Dionysian poetry.'

O'Hara drips:
'Lana Turner has collapsed!   326

I was trotting along and suddenly
it started raining and snowing
and you said it was hailing
but hailing hits you on the head
hard so it was really snowing and
raining and I was in such a hurry
to meet you but the traffic
was acting exactly like the sky
and suddenly I see a headline
LANA TURNER HAS COLLAPSED!
there is no snow in Hollywood
there is no rain in California'

Maneos sculpts:
'Smyrna is on fire!
I was with Sappho in Mytilene writing stormy poetry to the storied
lyra –
When suddenly Stavros stormed into the corner Taverna and
screamed:
'SMYRNA IS ON FIRE'
There is no dancing in Crete
There is no kissing in Corinth.'

O'Hara drips:
'The Israeli army is at the door and winged parachute-troopers   327
      rush around and nobody is scared while several die,
      among them a handsome stranger who had smiled and she
      had started loving.'

Maneos sculpts:
'The Persian army is trying to advance, yet the fair-haired Spartans
are slaughtering them as if they were small boys. Among the
bravest of the Spartans is comely Maron, son of Orsiphantus.'

O'Hara drips:
'it makes me very wistful, like reading a great Russian novel does'   328

Maneos sculpts:
'it makes me very pensive like reading a great Greek tragedy does.'

O'Hara drips:
'the Tartar hordes 329
are still advancing
and I identify with them'

Maneos sculpts:
'the Alemanni hordes
are still advancing –
But I will personally kill them all:
Let us show them that the men
they have plotted to murder are Romans,
and they themselves are barbarians!'

XXVII

O'Hara drips:
'It is almost three 330
I sit at the marble top
sorting poems, miserable
the little lamp glows feebly
I don't glow at all'

Maneos sculpts:
'It is exactly 3:23
I sit in the corner of Piazza S. Ignazio
Writing the proem for my collection of love poems.
I am as melancholy as an exiled star –
It is now 4:34.'

O'Hara drips:
'   I don't suppose I'll ever get 331
to Italy, but I have the terrible tundra at least.'

Maneos sculpts:
'I don't suppose I'll ever get
to Algeria, but at least I've seen much of Italy.'

O'Hara drips:
'
                              O the Polish summers! those drafts! 332
                              those black and white teeth!'

Maneos sculpts:
'O the Roman summers! Those wanton women!
Those black dresses, and raven tresses!'

O'Hara drips:
'It is 12:10 in New York and I am wondering   333
if I will finish this in time to meet Norman for lunch'

Maneos sculpts:
'It is 11:11 in Rome and I am wondering
if I will finish this in time to meet Flavia for a tryst,
or even a single kiss.'

O'Hara drips:
'It is 12:20 in New York a Friday   334
three days after Bastille day, yes
it is 1959 and I go get a shoeshine
because I will get off the 4:19 in Easthampton
at 7:15 and then go straight to dinner
and I don't know the people who will feed me'

Maneos sculpts:
'It is 12:12 in Rome, a Wednesday,
Four days before the floral Noantri Festival:
A festive carnival full of carnal color,
festooned allure, and colorful revelry.
It is 2002 – I am twenty-two –
Travelling on my self-designed Grand Tour
Imbibing every sign of ancient lore.'

O'Hara drips:
'The violent No! of the sun   335
burns the forehead of hills.
Sand fleas arrive from Salt Lake
and most of the theatres close.'

Maneos sculpts:
'The impassioned Yes! of The Italian Sun!
Is there anything more beautiful than being in beauteous Sorrento

on the balcony of Villa Lamaro,
bathing in the sun's searing glow
while listening to Dalaras sing *Sto pa kai sto ksanaleo*?'

O'Hara drips:
'   No. I wear workshirts to the opera,   336
often.'

Maneos sculpts:
'I often wear perfectly pressed Zegna suits to the opera.'

O'Hara drips:
'How funny you are today New York   337
Like Ginger Rogers in *Swingtime*
and St. Bridget's steeple leaning a little to the left'

Maneos sculpts:
'How passionate you are today, Rome –
Like Dionysus taunting Pentheus in Thebes,
Or Alpheus fighting at the fore against the whorish Medes.'

O'Hara drips:
'I wake up terrified and think   338
how much fun it would be to write a pornographic novel
immediately a cosmic man and woman are 69ing in the sky'

Maneos sculpts:
'I wake up overjoyed and think
how much fun it would be to write a decadent novel –
Immediately a Roman contessa
is smothered by kisses and caresses.'

O'Hara drips:
'   One need 339
never leave the confines of New York to get all the greenery one wishes-'

Maneos sculpts:
'One need never leave the confines of the Villa Borghese to get all the
greenery one wishes -'

O'Hara drips:
'   On   340
to Times Square, where the sign
blows smoke over my head,'

Maneos sculpts:
'On to the Villa Borghese where the statues inspire
like a newly found Homeric lyre.'

O'Hara drips:
'   this train is going away from the Guggenheim'   341

Maneos sculpts:
'The horses rest in the Villa Doria Pamphili'

O'Hara drips:
'Yesterday I felt very tired from being at the FIVE SPOT   342
and today I felt very tired from going to bed early and reading ULYSSES'

Maneos sculpts:
'Yesterday I felt ecstatic after being in the Domus Aurea
And today I felt elated after reading Dio Cassius'

O'Hara drips:
'meeting Roy and Bill I drink Vermouth   343
we talk about the pleasantness distractions of New York
you're almost there
57th Street'

Maneos sculpts:
'meeting Stelio and Alessandro, I drink Carmignano
we talk about the aesthetic decadence of Florence
we're almost there –
Palazzo Santo Spirito.'

O'Hara drips:
'515 Madison Avenue   344
door to heaven?'

Maneos sculpts:
'66 Piazza di Spagna
Door to Dante's second circle of hell?'

O'Hara drips:
'   when you   345
ride on a 5th Avenue bus you hide on a 5th
Avenue bus I mean compared to you walking'

Maneos sculpts:
'When you float idly upon a Venetian gondola
with a chestnut-tressed heiress
pressed to your chest –
the rest of existence ceases to exist.
For your only desire is to acquire a furious kiss –
A kiss as lovely and luxurious as an Italian idyll
Or a Pompeiian mural.'

O'Hara drips:
'and your brown lashes flutter revealing two perfect dawns colored   346
by New York'

Maneos sculpts:
'and your brown lashes flutter revealing two perfect suns colored by
Sardinian sea-fire.'

O'Hara drips:
'and back in New York Gregory is back in New York and we are   347
still missing each other in the Cedar and in hotel lobbies where Salvador
Dali is supposed to be asleep'

Maneos sculpts:
'Oh Rome! My true home!
City of Eternal Beauty! Country of Immortal Poetry!
Oh, how I've missed you so terribly!'

O'Hara drips:
'How exciting it is   348
                not to be at Port Lligat
or learning Portuguese in Bilbao so you can go to Brazil'

Maneos sculpts:
'How exciting it is
to be in Sorrento
learning Italian from an enamored *innamorata*'

O'Hara drips:
"I ate here with an Englishman

who ordered skate."

Maneos sculpts:
'I bloodied an Englishman
who smugly called Tuscany, Chiantishire:
'Is your blood choking you?'"

O'Hara drips:
'I'm going to New York!
(what a lark! what a song!)
where the tough Rocky's eaves
hit the sea. Where th'Acro-
polis is functional, the trains
that run and shout! the books
that have trousers and sleeves!

I'm going to New York!
(quel voyage! jamais plus!)
far from Ypsilanti and Flint!
where Goodman rules the Empire
and the sunlight's eschato-
logy upon the wizard's bridges
and the galleries of print!

I'm going to New York!
(to my friends! mes semblables!)
I suppose I'll walk back West.
But for now I'm gone forever!
the city's hung with flashlights!
the Ferry's unbuttoning its vest!'

Maneos sculpts:

'I'm going to Magna Graecia!
Catania, Sicilia
To be precise.
'The Beautiful Land!'
So very far from Manhattan
and from London, England.

I'm going to Magna Graecia!
Ah, the isles of Sicily!
Favignana – Linosa and Lampedusa.
The very lifeblood of ancient Poetry!
Let me come
to be one
with your illustrious Beauty.

I'm going to Magna Graecia!
Oh, dark-skinned daughters of Sicilia:
Children of the once mighty Moors.
Whose glances are stolen from Tosca,
slayer of craven Scarpia.
And whose kisses are like winged daggers
dripping with the flowing blood of Aetna:
Savage and primal –
Full of scalding Lava,
Yet somehow still irresistible!

Oh, my Sicily!
A tiny glimpse of timeless Grecian Glory!
A muted glimmer of fallen Roman Beauty!'

O'Hara drips:
'Only you in New York are not boring tonight'   352

Maneos sculpts:
'Only you in Taormina are not boring tonight'

O'Hara drips:
'Don't tell me to smile, oh flamboyant egrets! not   353
while I'm pining naked on the Spanish Steps'

Maneos sculpts:
'Don't bother me with petty American politics.
Not while I'm composing purple prose,
surrounded by ravishing, radiant roses,
on the Spanish Steps.'

O'Hara drips:
'As I walked into the Dairy B & H Lunch I couldn't remember   354
your other eye, I puked.'

Maneos sculpts:
'As we walked through the Villa D'Este
talking of poppies and poetry,
I kissed her breast.'

O'Hara drips:
'Ah nuts!'   355

Maneos sculpts:
'Porca Miseria!'

O'Hara drips:
'the Empire I am most interested in is Han'   356

Maneos sculpts:
'the Empire I am most interested in is Rome'

XXVIII

O'Hara drips:
'The sad thing about life is   357
that I need money to write poetry
and If I am a good poet
nobody will care how I got it
and If I am a bad poet
nobody will know how I got it'

Maneos sculpts:
'How much longer can I

write such Immortal Poetry
in such abject poverty?'

O'Hara drips:
'My eyes are vague blue, like the sky, and change all the time;'   358

Maneos sculpts:
'My eyes are fire-red, like the Indian Sun, and blaze all the time'

O'Hara drips:
'
                              While I was writing 359
it I was realizing that if I wanted to I could use the telephone instead of
writing the poem,'

Maneos sculpts:
'While editing my Satire, I realized that no matter how tired I was, I
must continue working.'

O'Hara drips:
'Isn't it enough to be middle-age   360
and French? do we have to be sage?"

Maneos sculpts:
'Isn't it enough to be middle-aged and impeccably beautiful?
Why must one be economically useful?'

O'Hara drips:
'Boom of pregnant hillsides   361
awash with urine'

Maneos sculpts:
'Boom of blooming hillocks
Bursting with everlasting, everblooming hollyhock.'

O'Hara drips:
'I remember Moscow   362
I remember two herdsmen in fur caps
and they were lying down together'

Maneos sculpts:

'I remember Granada
I remember two gypsies wrapped in long robes,
And they were singing an Arab lament to the lambent Andalusian
moon.'

O'Hara drips:
'   All   363
night I sit on the outspread knees
of addicts; their kindness
makes them talk like whores to
the sun as it moves me hysterically
forward. The subway shoots onto a ramp
overlooking the East River, the towers!
the minarets! The bridge. I'm lost.'

Maneos sculpts:
'All night I delight
in the delicate moonlight
falling into the harbor of Gibraltar.
A light kissed with amor-kissed
amaryllis,
And threaded with quicksilver stolen
from the amaranthine Sun.
Oh, for the bloodlust of the gypsy moon!
Oh, for the throbbing of the heady stars!
I am found!'

O'Hara drips:
'You preferred the Arabs? but they didn't stay to count   364
their inventions, racing into sands, converting themselves into
so many,
   embracing, at Ramadan, the tenderest effigies of
themselves with penises shorn by the hundreds, like a camel
ravishing a goat.'

Maneos sculpts:
'*Habibi, ya nour el ain!*   365
I loved the Arabs before they were infected with radical Islam,
plagued with an insular, medieval view of the world – pure evil!

Free yourselves, my Arab friends, from these anvils!

So now, my fellow Americans, let us be thankful that we are free
from the Asiatic slavery,
flowing from the minaret of El-Mursi.
And let us fight to the bitter end to defend the timeless tenets of our
Democracy.
And if you don't believe me
listen to the very words spoken by Shahzad, our avowed enemy!
Islam will spread on the whole word, and the democracy will be 366
defeated
As so was communism, and all the other isms and schisms be defeated
And the word of Allah will be supreme, inshallah.'

O'Hara drips:
'Am I to become profligate as if I were a blonde?' 367

Maneos sculpts:
'Am I to become profligate as if I were Tiberius?'

O'Hara drips:
'And the most beautiful jungle of madness being sent 368
and sent! and sent! and sent! and sent! into oblivion
is the great sensual blinking flag of alarm at night
hearing itself stuffed and hung, as the stars "hear" longing.
In the darkness I am growing larger!
In the darkness I am growing louder!
I am swinging and clanging inside myself like the tongue of a bell!'

Maneos sculpts:
'Under Arcadian trees, I am dangling dangerously on the precipice of
madness.
Dancing with my thyrsus, I am hypnotically singing the dying hymns
of Dionysus,
while giving countless kisses to my boundless devotees: my maenads,
my satyrs and my maidens.
Amidst all of this riotous revelry, and against the lush wishes of my
plush harems,
I must now object to Modern Versifying!
Pan, my friends, is living!

Pulsing, Pounding and Palpitating with Life!'

O'Hara drips:
'If I'd been in Berlin in
1930, would I have seen you
ambling the streets like
Krazy Kat?'

369

Maneos sculpts:
'If I'd been in Berlin in 1933
I'd have attempted to free Germany
from the Nazi's deadly decrees.
For death is softer by far than Tyranny.
And nothing holds more glory,
than in dying for Love or Liberty.'

O'Hara drips:
'And at night a truce
with Iran or Korea seems certain
while I am beaten to death
by a thug in a back bedroom.'

370

Maneos sculpts:
'The Syrians are heroically
dying for Freedom.
And what am I doing?
Posing – and composing
minor Poetry.
And as I dally,
the remains of Tyranny
are slowly withering
like frost when
caressed by the carnal breast of the Sun.
Oh, if only I could take Action,
if only I could *bleed* with such Men!'

O'Hara drips:
'oh god it's wonderful
to get out of bed
and drink too much coffee

371

and smoke too many cigarettes
and love you so much'

Maneos sculpts:
'Oh god it's so wonderful
to slip into a wondrous bed –
To drink too much espresso –
And to take too many lusty lovers.'

O'Hara drips:
'I am the least difficult of men. All I want is boundless love.'   372

Maneos sculpts:
'I am the most difficult of men, for I crave boundless love.'

O'Hara drips:
'   I don't think I want to win anything I think I want to   373
die unadorned'

Maneos sculpts:
'I think that I wish to be crowned with wild-kisses and wild-parsley in
Rome, Alexandria, or Ephesus.'

O'Hara drips:
'   I don't think of fame or posterity (as Keats so grandly and   374
genuinely did),'

Maneos sculpts:
'I think I shall be among the Grecian pantheon after my death.'

XXIX

My song has ceased –
For I have stated my poetic peace
In a rather lengthy piece.
But my Satire is truly done.
My quill's fierce Will has been run.

I have attacked hacks one day and Nobel laureates the next.
But I have always protected

The Beautiful from literary-schools and barbaric fools.
Some even say that I have triumphed in my intellectual duel.

WORKS CITED (NOTES)

AUTHOR'S INTRODUCTION

1. Maneos, Pietros. "American Bards & The London Reviewer: A Satire."

2. Maneos, Pietros. "American Bards & The London Reviewer: A Satire."

3. Swinburne, Algernon Charles. "Hymn to Prosperine." Line 86. *Poems and Ballads & Atalanta in Calydon.* Kenneth Haynes. New York: Penguin Books, 2000. Page 59.

4. Swinburne, Algernon Charles. "Sapphics." Line 45. *Poems and Ballads & Atalanta in Calydon.* Kenneth Haynes. New York: Penguin Books, 2000. Page 164.

5. Eliot, T.S. "The Love Song of J. Alfred Prufrock." Line 111. *The Complete Poems and Plays: 1909-1950.* New York: Harcourt Brace & Company, 1980. Page 7.

6. Maneos, Pietros. "American Bards & The London Reviewer: A Satire."

7. Cavafy, C.P. "Thermopylae." Line 14. *The Complete Poems of Cavafy.* Translated by Rae Dalven, Introduction by W.H. Auden. New York: Harcourt Brace & Company, 1989. Page 9.

T.S. ELIOT SECTION

8. Eliot, T.S. "The Love Song of J. Alfred Prufrock." Lines 111-114. *The Complete Poems and Plays: 1909-1950.* New York: Harcourt Brace & Company, 1980. Page 7.

9. Eliot, T.S. Introductory Quotation to "The Wasteland." Translated by Nick Mount in this particular lecture: http://www.channels.com/episodes/show/12682184/Nick-Mount-on-T-S-Eliot-s-The-Waste-Land.

10. Eliot, T.S. "Gerontion." Lines 1-4. *The Complete Poems and Plays: 1909-1950.* New York: Harcourt Brace & Company, 1980. Page 21.

11. Eliot, T.S. "Gerontion." Lines 57-60. *The Complete Poems and Plays: 1909-1950.* New York: Harcourt Brace & Company, 1980. Page 23.

12. Eliot, T.S. "Four Quartets: East Coker." Lines 98-101. *The Complete Poems and Plays: 1909-1950.* New York: Harcourt Brace & Company, 1980. Page 126.

13. Homer, "The Iliad." Book IX. Lines 383-386. Translated by Robert Fitzgerald. Introduction by G.S. Kirk. New York: Oxford University Press, 1998. Page 154.

14. Homer, "The Odyssey." Book XXII. Lines 61-64. Introduction and Translation by Richmond Lattimore. New York: Harper Perennial, 1999. Page 322.

15. Plutarch, *Plutarch on Sparta.* Translated by Richard Talbert. New York: Penguin Books, 1988. Page 146.

16. Herodotus, *The Histories.* Stanza 226. Translated by Robin Waterfield. New York: Oxford University Press, 1998. Pages 483-484.

17. Aeschylus' epitaph.

18. Livy, *The Rise of Rome: Books 1-5.* Book 2, Chapter 11-12. Translated by T.J. Luce. New York: Oxford University Press, 1998. Page 83.

19. Paroulakis, Peter. *The Greek War of Independence.* Darwin, Australia: Hellenic International Press, 2000. Page 93.

20. Ioannis Metaxas' reply 'Oxi' (No) to Mussolini's occupational demands.

21. Seal Team Six is the elite unit of Navy Seals that killed Osama Bin Laden in Abbottabad, Pakistan on May 2nd, 2011. The particular phrase 'Geronimo EKIA' was the first verbal confirmation that Osama Bin Laden, code-named Geronimo, had been killed by this unit. EKIA is the acronym for 'Enemy Killed In Action.'

22. Eliot, T.S. "The Hollow Men." Lines 1-10. *The Complete Poems and Plays: 1909-1950.* New York: Harcourt Brace & Company, 1980. Page 56.

23. Eliot, T.S. "The Hollow Men." Lines 15-18. *The Complete Poems and Plays: 1909-1950.* New York: Harcourt Brace & Company, 1980. Page 56.

24. Eliot, T.S. "The Love Song of J. Alfred Prufrock." Lines 83-86. *The Complete Poems and Plays: 1909-1950.* New York: Harcourt Brace & Company, 1980. Page 6.

25. Eliot, T.S. "In silent corridors of death." Lines 10-14. *Inventions of the March Hare: Poems 1909-1917.* New York: Harcourt Brace & Company, 1998. Page 93.

26. Eliot, T.S. "Four Quartets: Little Gidding" Lines 128-130. *The Complete Poems and Plays: 1909-1950.* New York: Harcourt Brace & Company, 1980. Page 141.

27. Eliot, T.S. "Burbank with a Baedeker: Bleistein with a Cigar." Lines 5-8. *The Complete Poems and Plays: 1909-1950.* New York: Harcourt Brace & Company, 1980. Page 24.

28. Eliot, T.S. "Hysteria" Lines 7-12. *The Complete Poems and Plays: 1909-1950.* New York: Harcourt Brace & Company, 1980. Page 19.

29. Eliot, T.S. "The Love Song of J. Alfred Prufrock." Lines 37-40. *The Complete Poems and Plays: 1909-1950.* New York: Harcourt Brace & Company, 1980. Page 4.

30. Eliot, T.S. "The Wasteland." Lines 185-186. *The Complete Poems and Plays: 1909-1950.* New York: Harcourt Brace & Company, 1980. Page 43.

31. Eliot, T.S. "Gerontion." Lines 8-10. *The Complete Poems and Plays: 1909-1950.* New York: Harcourt Brace & Company, 1980. Page 21.

32. Eliot, T.S. "Goldfish (Essence of Summer Magazines) Embarquement pour Cythere (II)." Line 15. *Inventions of the March Hare: Poems 1909-1917.* New York: Harcourt Brace & Company, 1998. Page 27.

33. Eliot, T.S. "The Wasteland." Lines 1-7. *The Complete Poems and Plays: 1909-1950.* New York: Harcourt Brace & Company, 1980. Page 37.

34. Eliot, T.S. "Murder in the Cathedral." Lines 9-11. *The Complete Poems and Plays: 1909-1950.* New York: Harcourt Brace & Company, 1980. Page 175.

35. Eliot, T.S. "Preludes." Lines 1-3. *The Complete Poems and Plays: 1909-1950.* New York: Harcourt Brace & Company, 1980. Page 12.

36. Eliot, T.S. "Preludes." Lines 14-18. *The Complete Poems and Plays: 1909-1950.* New York: Harcourt Brace & Company, 1980. Page 12.

37. Eliot, T.S. "Second Caprice in North Cambridge." Lines 1-3. *Inventions of the March Hare: Poems 1909-1917.* New York: Harcourt Brace & Company, 1998. Page 15.

38. Eliot, T.S. "The Wasteland." Lines 266-267. *The Complete Poems and Plays: 1909-1950.* New York: Harcourt Brace & Company, 1980. Page 45.

39. Eliot, T.S. "The Wasteland." Lines 115-116. *The Complete Poems and Plays: 1909-1950.* New York: Harcourt Brace & Company, 1980. Page 40.

40. Eliot, T.S. "Burbank with a Baedeker: Bleistein with a Cigar." Lines 22-24. *The Complete Poems and Plays: 1909-1950.* New York: Harcourt Brace & Company, 1980. Page 24.

41. Eliot, T.S. "The Wasteland." Lines 187-189. *The Complete Poems and Plays: 1909-1950.* New York: Harcourt Brace & Company, 1980. Page 43.

42. Eliot, T.S. "The Hollow Men." Lines 39-44. *The Complete Poems and Plays: 1909-1950.* New York: Harcourt Brace & Company, 1980. Page 57.

43. Eliot, T.S. "Five-Finger Exercises: Lines to a Yorkshire Terrier." Lines 11-15. *The Complete Poems and Plays: 1909-1950.* New York: Harcourt Brace & Company, 1980. Page 91.

44. Eliot, T.S. "The Four Quartets: Little Gidding." Lines 10-20. *The Complete Poems and Plays: 1909-1950.* New York: Harcourt Brace & Company, 1980. Page 138.

45. Eliot, T.S. "The Wasteland" Lines 22-30. *The Complete Poems and Plays: 1909-1950.* New York: Harcourt Brace & Company, 1980. Page 38.

46. Eliot, T.S. "Rhapsody on a Windy Night." Lines 8-12. *The Complete Poems and Plays: 1909-1950.* New York: Harcourt Brace & Company, 1980. Page 14.

47. Eliot, T.S. "Easter: Sensations of April (I)." Lines 4-12. *Inventions of the March Hare: Poems 1909-1917*. New York: Harcourt Brace & Company, 1998. Page 23.

48. Eliot, T.S. "Easter: Sensations of April (II)." Lines 1-10. *Inventions of the March Hare: Poems 1909-1917*. New York: Harcourt Brace & Company, 1998. Page 24.

49. Eliot, T.S. "Rhapsody on a Windy Night." Lines 50-53. *The Complete Poems and Plays: 1909-1950*. New York: Harcourt Brace & Company, 1980. Page 15.

50. Eliot, T.S. "The Four Quartets: Little Gidding." Lines 66-71. *The Complete Poems and Plays: 1909-1950*. New York: Harcourt Brace & Company, 1980. Page 140.

51. Eliot, T.S. "Goldfish (Essence of Summer Magazines) (III)." Lines 1-5. *Inventions of the March Hare: Poems 1909-1917*. New York: Harcourt Brace & Company, 1998. Page 28.

52. Eliot, T.S. "Preludes." Lines 9-13. *The Complete Poems and Plays: 1909-1950*. New York: Harcourt Brace & Company, 1980. Page 12.

53. Eliot, T.S. "The Wasteland" Lines 259-263. *The Complete Poems and Plays: 1909-1950*. New York: Harcourt Brace & Company, 1980. Page 45.

54. Eliot, T.S. "The Love Song of J. Alfred Prufrock." Lines 70-74. *The Complete Poems and Plays: 1909-1950*. New York: Harcourt Brace & Company, 1980. Page 5.

55. Eliot, T.S. "The Wasteland" Lines 9-12. *The Complete Poems and Plays: 1909-1950*. New York: Harcourt Brace & Company, 1980. Page 37.

56. This phrase 'I was born a Greek, I shall die a Greek' was spoken by Athanasios Diakos, the Grecian hero from the 19th century Revolution against the Ottomans, to Omer Vryonis, the barbarian commander. After being captured and brought before Vryonis, Vryonis offered to make Diakos a captain in the Ottoman Army if he converted to Islam. Diakos refused and uttered the above statement, which is transliterated as 'Ego Graikos yennithika, Graikos the na pethano.' Once refusing Vryonis offer, Diakos was impaled and roasted alive. (http://en.wikipedia.org/wiki/Athanasios_Diakos)

57. Eliot, T.S. "The Love Song of J. Alfred Prufrock." Line 122. *The Complete Poems and Plays: 1909-1950*. New York: Harcourt Brace & Company, 1980. Page 7.

58. Eliot, T.S. "Interlude in London." Lines 1-3. *Inventions of the March Hare: Poems 1909-1917*. New York: Harcourt Brace & Company, 1998. Page 16.

59. Eliot, T.S. "Preludes." Lines 21-23. *The Complete Poems and Plays: 1909-1950*. New York: Harcourt Brace & Company, 1980. Page 12.

60. Eliot, T.S. "The Hollow Men." Lines 31-33. *The Complete Poems and Plays: 1909-1950*. New York: Harcourt Brace & Company, 1980. Page 57.

61. Eliot, T.S. "The Wasteland" Lines 174-175. *The Complete Poems and Plays: 1909-1950*. New York: Harcourt Brace & Company, 1980. Page 42.

62. Eliot, T.S. "The Wasteland" Line 182. *The Complete Poems and Plays: 1909-1950*. New York: Harcourt Brace & Company, 1980. Page 42.

63. Eliot, T.S. "Preludes." Lines 52-54. *The Complete Poems and Plays: 1909-1950*. New York: Harcourt Brace & Company, 1980. Page 13.

64. Eliot, T.S. "The Wasteland" Lines 207-214. *The Complete Poems and Plays: 1909-1950*. New York: Harcourt Brace & Company, 1980. Page 43.

65. Eliot, T.S. "The Wasteland" Lines 193-198. *The Complete Poems and Plays: 1909-1950*. New York: Harcourt Brace & Company, 1980. Page 43.

66. Eliot, T.S. "The Wasteland" Lines 69-76. *The Complete Poems and Plays: 1909-1950*. New York: Harcourt Brace & Company, 1980. Page 39.

67. Homer, "The Odyssey." Book XVII. Lines 322-328. Introduction and Translation by Richmond Lattimore. New York: Harper Perennial, 1999. Page 261.

68. Eliot, T.S. "Gerontion." Lines 19-20. *The Complete Poems and Plays: 1909-1950*. New York: Harcourt Brace & Company, 1980. Page 21.

69. Eliot, T.S. "Choruses from The Rock." VIII. *The Complete Poems and Plays: 1909-1950.* New York: Harcourt Brace & Company, 1980. Page 109.

70. Eliot, T.S. "Untitled." Lines 1-4. *Inventions of the March Hare: Poems 1909-1917.* New York: Harcourt Brace & Company, 1998. Page 83.

71. Eliot, T.S. "Choruses from The Rock." III. *The Complete Poems and Plays: 1909-1950.* New York: Harcourt Brace & Company, 1980. Page 104.

72. Eliot, T.S. "The Four Quartets: Little Gidding." Lines 168-170. *The Complete Poems and Plays: 1909-1950.* New York: Harcourt Brace & Company, 1980. Pages 142-143.

73. Eliot, T.S. "Choruses from The Rock." III. *The Complete Poems and Plays: 1909-1950.* New York: Harcourt Brace & Company, 1980. Page 102.

74. Eliot, T.S. "Choruses from The Rock." IX. *The Complete Poems and Plays: 1909-1950.* New York: Harcourt Brace & Company, 1980. Page 110.

75. Eliot, T.S. "Choruses from The Rock." V. *The Complete Poems and Plays: 1909-1950.* New York: Harcourt Brace & Company, 1980. Page 105.

76. Eliot, T.S. "Choruses from The Rock." VII. *The Complete Poems and Plays: 1909-1950.* New York: Harcourt Brace & Company, 1980. Page 108.

77. Eliot, T.S. "Choruses from The Rock." VIII. *The Complete Poems and Plays: 1909-1950.* New York: Harcourt Brace & Company, 1980. Page 109.

78. Eliot, T.S. "The Love Song of J. Alfred Prufrock." Lines 87-95. *The Complete Poems and Plays: 1909-1950.* New York: Harcourt Brace & Company, 1980. Page 6.

79. 'Vicisti Galilaee' is translated 'You have won, Galilean' which is often falsely attributed as the last words of Julian, The Hellenist (I will not impugn his character by titling him Julian, The Apostate, as others have done). The second line, 'Sed anima Dios adhuc intra me vivit, Galilaee' is translated as 'But the soul of Zeus still lives within me, Galilean.' I would like to thank the Classicist Carrie Mowbray from the University of Pennsylvania for her gracious assistance with this passage.

80. Eliot, T.S. "The Wasteland." Lines 300-304. *The Complete Poems and Plays: 1909-1950.* New York: Harcourt Brace & Company, 1980. Page 46.

81. Eliot, T.S. "Mandarins, II." Lines 1-2. *Inventions of the March Hare: Poems 1909-1917.* New York: Harcourt Brace & Company, 1998. Page 20.

82. Eliot, T.S. "The Wasteland." Lines 61-63. *The Complete Poems and Plays: 1909-1950.* New York: Harcourt Brace & Company, 1980. Page 39.

83. Eliot, T.S. "The Boston Evening Transcript." Lines 1-2. *The Complete Poems and Plays: 1909-1950.* New York: Harcourt Brace & Company, 1980. Page 16.

84. Eliot, T.S. "Choruses from The Rock." I. *The Complete Poems and Plays: 1909-1950.* New York: Harcourt Brace & Company, 1980. Page 96.

85. Eliot, T.S. "The Wasteland." Lines 60-68. *The Complete Poems and Plays: 1909-1950.* New York: Harcourt Brace & Company, 1980. Page 39.

86. Eliot, T.S. "The Four Quartets: Burnt Norton." Lines 113-116. *The Complete Poems and Plays: 1909-1950.* New York: Harcourt Brace & Company, 1980. Page 120.

87. Eliot, T.S. "The Hollow Men." Lines 52-60. *The Complete Poems and Plays: 1909-1950.* New York: Harcourt Brace & Company, 1980. Page 56.

88. Eliot, T.S. "Entretien dans un parc." Lines 26-27. *Inventions of the March Hare: Poems 1909-1917.* New York: Harcourt Brace & Company, 1998. Page 16.

89. Eliot, T.S. "The Love Song of J. Alfred Prufrock." Line 129-131. *The Complete Poems and Plays: 1909-1950.* New York: Harcourt Brace & Company, 1980. Page 7.

90. Eliot, T.S. "The Naming of Cats." Lines 1-4. *The Complete Poems and Plays: 1909-1950.* New York: Harcourt Brace & Company, 1980. Page 149.

91. Eliot, T.S. "The Wasteland." Lines 168-171. *The Complete Poems and Plays: 1909-1950*. New York: Harcourt Brace & Company, 1980. Page 42.

92. Eliot, T.S. "The Wasteland." Lines 183-184. *The Complete Poems and Plays: 1909-1950*. New York: Harcourt Brace & Company, 1980. Page 42.

93. Eliot, T.S. "The Wasteland." Lines 31-34. *The Complete Poems and Plays: 1909-1950*. New York: Harcourt Brace & Company, 1980. Page 38.

94. Puccini, Giacomo. "Che Gelida Manina." *La Boheme.* The translation is 'Who am I? I am a poet/What do I do? I write./And how do I live? I live./In my happy poverty, I am a prince who squanders arias and couplets of longing.'

95. Eliot, T.S. "Whispers of Immortality." Lines 1-4. *The Complete Poems and Plays: 1909-1950*. New York: Harcourt Brace & Company, 1980. Page 32.

96. Eliot, T.S. "A Cooking Egg." Lines 1-4. *The Complete Poems and Plays: 1909-1950*. New York: Harcourt Brace & Company, 1980. Page 26.

97. Eliot, T.S. "A Cooking Egg." Lines 9-12. *The Complete Poems and Plays: 1909-1950*. New York: Harcourt Brace & Company, 1980. Page 27.

98. Eliot, T.S. "A Cooking Egg." Lines 13-16. *The Complete Poems and Plays: 1909-1950*. New York: Harcourt Brace & Company, 1980. Page 27.

99. Eliot, T.S. "A Cooking Egg." Lines 17-20. *The Complete Poems and Plays: 1909-1950*. New York: Harcourt Brace & Company, 1980. Page 27.

100. Eliot, T.S. "A Cooking Egg." Lines 21-24. *The Complete Poems and Plays: 1909-1950*. New York: Harcourt Brace & Company, 1980. Page 27.

101. Eliot, T.S. "Mr. Apollinax." Lines 1-5. *The Complete Poems and Plays: 1909-1950*. New York: Harcourt Brace & Company, 1980. Page 18.

102. Eliot, T.S. "The Wasteland." Lines 218-221. *The Complete Poems and Plays: 1909-1950*. New York: Harcourt Brace & Company, 1980. Pages 43-44.

103. Eliot, T.S. "The Wasteland." Lines 228-234. *The Complete Poems and Plays: 1909-1950*. New York: Harcourt Brace & Company, 1980. Page 44.

104. Eliot, T.S. "Cousin Nancy." Lines 1-10. *The Complete Poems and Plays: 1909-1950*. New York: Harcourt Brace & Company, 1980. Page 17.

105. Eliot, T.S. "Portrait of a Lady." Lines 122-124. *The Complete Poems and Plays: 1909-1950*. New York: Harcourt Brace & Company, 1980. Page 11.

106. Eliot, T.S. "The Four Quartets: East Coker." Lines 174-178. *The Complete Poems and Plays: 1909-1950*. New York: Harcourt Brace & Company, 1980. Page 128.

107. Eliot, T.S. "Portrait of a Lady." Lines 106-108. *The Complete Poems and Plays: 1909-1950*. New York: Harcourt Brace & Company, 1980. Page 11.

108. Eliot, T.S. "Portrait of a Lady." Lines 58-60. *The Complete Poems and Plays: 1909-1950*. New York: Harcourt Brace & Company, 1980. Page 9.

109. Eliot, T.S. "The Love Song of J. Alfred Prufrock." Lines 114-119. *The Complete Poems and Plays: 1909-1950*. New York: Harcourt Brace & Company, 1980. Page 7.

110. Eliot, T.S.. "Letter to Athenaeum." *The Letters of T.S. Eliot Volume I 1898-1922*. Edited by Valerie Eliot. New York: Harcourt Brace Jovanovich, 1988. Page 387.

111. Eliot, T.S. "The Wasteland." Line 393. *The Complete Poems and Plays: 1909-1950*. New York: Harcourt Brace & Company, 1980. Page 49.

112. Eliot, T.S. "The Wasteland." Lines 142-149. *The Complete Poems and Plays: 1909-1950*. New York: Harcourt Brace & Company, 1980. Page 41.

113. Eliot, T.S.. "Letter to James Joyce." *The Letters of T.S. Eliot Volume I 1898-1922*. Edited by Valerie Eliot. New York: Harcourt Brace Jovanovich, 1988. Page 455.

114. Eliot, T.S. "The Love Song of J. Alfred Prufrock." Lines 13-14. *The Complete Poems and Plays: 1909-1950*. New York: Harcourt Brace & Company, 1980. Page 4.

115. Eliot, T.S. "Gerontion." Lines 15-16. *The Complete Poems and Plays: 1909-1950*. New York: Harcourt Brace & Company, 1980. Page 21.

116. Eliot, T.S. "The Love Song of J. Alfred Prufrock." Line 51. *The Complete Poems and Plays: 1909-1950*. New York: Harcourt Brace & Company, 1980. Page 5.

117. Eliot, T.S. "The Four Quartets: East Coker." Lines 137-139. *The Complete Poems and Plays: 1909-1950*. New York: Harcourt Brace & Company, 1980. Page 127.

118. Eliot, T.S. "The Love Song of J. Alfred Prufrock." Lines 45-46. *The Complete Poems and Plays: 1909-1950*. New York: Harcourt Brace & Company, 1980. Page 4-5.

119. Eliot, T.S. "Portrait of a Lady." Lines 50-51. *The Complete Poems and Plays: 1909-1950*. New York: Harcourt Brace & Company, 1980. Page 9.

120. Eliot, T.S. "Portrait of a Lady." Line 68. *The Complete Poems and Plays: 1909-1950*. New York: Harcourt Brace & Company, 1980. Page 10.

121. Eliot, T.S. "The Love Song of J. Alfred Prufrock." Lines 119-120. *The Complete Poems and Plays: 1909-1950*. New York: Harcourt Brace & Company, 1980. Page 7.

122. Eliot, T.S. "Opera." Lines 12-13. *Inventions of the March Hare: Poems 1909-1917*. New York: Harcourt Brace & Company, 1998. Page 17.

123. Eliot, T.S. "In the Department Store." Lines 7-8. *Inventions of the March Hare: Poems 1909-1917*. New York: Harcourt Brace & Company, 1998. Page 56.

124. Eliot, T.S. "Five-Finger Exercises: Lines to a Persian Cat." Line 6-10. *The Complete Poems and Plays: 1909-1950*. New York: Harcourt Brace & Company, 1980. Page 91.

125. Eliot, T.S. "The Four Quartets: East Coker." Lines 102-104. *The Complete Poems and Plays: 1909-1950*. New York: Harcourt Brace & Company, 1980. Page 126.

126. Eliot, T.S. "The Hollow Men." Lines 94-97. *The Complete Poems and Plays: 1909-1950*. New York: Harcourt Brace & Company, 1980. Page 59.

CHARLES BUKOWSKI SECTION

127. Bukowski, Charles. "ill." Lines 28-29. *The Last Night of the Earth Poems*. Santa Rosa, California: Black Sparrow Press, 1992. Page 190.

128. Bukowski, Charles. "beds, toilets, you and me-" Lines 1-4. *Love is a Dog From Hell*. Santa Rosa, California: Black Sparrow Press, 2002. Page 132.

129. Bukowski, Charles. "Part 2" Lines 1-2. *Sifting Through The Madness For The Word, The Line, The Way: New Poems*. Edited by John Martin. New York: Harper Collins Publishers, 2003. Page 107.

130. Bukowski, Charles. "this." Lines 57-59. *The Last Night of the Earth Poems*. Santa Rosa, California: Black Sparrow Press, 1992. Page 135.

131. Bukowski, Charles. "blasted apart with the first breath." Lines 25-28. *The Last Night of the Earth Poems*. Santa Rosa, California: Black Sparrow Press, 1992. Page 148.

132. Bukowski, Charles. "hug the dark." Lines 27-30. *Play The Piano Drunk Like A Percussion Instrument Until The Fingers Begin To Bleed A Bit*. Santa Rosa, California: Black Sparrow Press, 2001. Page 113.

133. Bukowski, Charles. "the man with the beautiful eyes." Lines 40-45. *The Last Night of the Earth Poems*. Santa Rosa, California: Black Sparrow Press, 1992. Page 45.

134. Bukowski, Charles. "hunk of rock." Lines 18-21. *The Last Night of the Earth Poems*. Santa Rosa, California: Black Sparrow Press, 1992. Page 86.

135. Bukowski, Charles. "hunk of rock." Lines 53-54. *The Last Night of the Earth Poems*. Santa Rosa, California: Black Sparrow Press, 1992. Page 87

136. Bukowski, Charles. "torched-out." Lines 132-137. *The Last Night of the Earth Poems*. Santa Rosa, California: Black Sparrow Press, 1992. Page 384

137. Bukowski, Charles. "high school girls." Lines 19-24. *Slouching Toward Nirvana: New Poems.* Edited by John Martin. New York: Harper Collins Publishers, 2005. Page 113.

138. Bukowski, Charles. "john dillinger and *le chasseur maudit*." Lines 2-6. *Burning in Water Drowning in Flame.* Santa Barbara, California: Black Sparrow Press, 1985. Page 132.

139. Bukowski, Charles. "before Aids." Lines 1-10. *The Last Night of the Earth Poems.* Santa Rosa, California: Black Sparrow Press, 1992. Page 83.

140. Bukowski, Charles. "the feel of it." Lines 56-59. *The Last Night of the Earth Poems.* Santa Rosa, California: Black Sparrow Press, 1992. Page 32.

141. Bukowski, Charles. "confession." Lines 1-4. *The Last Night of the Earth Poems.* Santa Rosa, California: Black Sparrow Press, 1992. Page 138.

142. Bukowski, Charles. "class." Lines 15-20. *Burning in Water Drowning in Flame.* Santa Barbara, California: Black Sparrow Press, 1985. Page 116.

143. Bukowski, Charles. "Untitled." Lines 1-3. *Play The Piano Drunk Like A Percussion Instrument Until The Fingers Begin To Bleed A Bit.* Santa Rosa, California: Black Sparrow Press, 2001. Page 7.

144. Bukowski, Charles. "the greatest actor of our day." Lines 91-99. *The Last Night of the Earth Poems.* Santa Rosa, California: Black Sparrow Press, 1992. Page 36.

145. Bukowski, Charles. "the bird." Lines 16-20. *Burning in Water Drowning in Flame.* Santa Barbara, California: Black Sparrow Press, 1985. Page 44.

146. Bukowski, Charles. "the twins." Lines 40-43. *Burning in Water Drowning in Flame.* Santa Barbara, California: Black Sparrow Press, 1985. Page 24.

147. Bukowski, Charles. "the automobiles of DeLongpre." Lines 27-28. *The Night Torn Mad With Footsteps: New Poems.* New York: Harper Collins Publishers, 2003. Page 65.

148. Bukowski, Charles. "the singular shelf." Lines 30-31. *Burning in Water Drowning in Flame.* Santa Barbara, California: Black Sparrow Press, 1985. Page 45.

149. Bukowski, Charles. "old poet." Lines 7-8. *Burning in Water Drowning in Flame.* Santa Barbara, California: Black Sparrow Press, 1985. Page 29.

150. Uttered by Bukowski during an interview. See http://youtu.be/MHRcKjvX1xE, 0:50 to 1:07.

151. Bukowski, Charles. "T.M." Lines 14-17. *Love is a Dog From Hell.* Santa Rosa, California: Black Sparrow Press, 2002. Page 53.

152. Cavafy, C.P. "Antony's Ending." Line 15-16. *C.P. Cavafy Collected Poems.* Translated by Edmund Keeley and Phillip Sherrard. Edited by George Savidis. Princeton, New Jersey: Princeton University Press, 1992. Page 194.

153. Bukowski, Charles. "gloomy lady" Lines 39-43. *Love is a Dog From Hell.* Santa Rosa, California: Black Sparrow Press, 2002. Page 104.

154. Bukowski, Charles. "untitled." Lines 1-4. *Burning in Water Drowning in Flame.* Santa Barbara, California: Black Sparrow Press, 1985. Page 96.

155. Bukowski, Charles. "guru" Lines 44-48. *Love is a Dog From Hell.* Santa Rosa, California: Black Sparrow Press, 2002. Page 86.

156. Bukowski, Charles. "young in New Orleans." Lines 4-5. *The Last Night of the Earth Poems.* Santa Rosa, California: Black Sparrow Press, 1992. Page 353

157. Bukowski, Charles. "Bolero." Lines 16-17. *Slouching Toward Nirvana: New Poems.* Edited by John Martin. New York: Harper Collins Publishers, 2005. Page 31.

158. Bukowski, Charles. "I fought them from the moment I saw light." Lines 64-65. *Slouching Toward Nirvana: New Poems.* Edited by John Martin. New York: Harper Collins Publishers, 2005. Page 186.

159. Bukowski, Charles. "the crunch." Lines 34-42. *Love is a Dog From Hell.* Santa Rosa, California: Black Sparrow Press, 2002. Page 163.

160. Bukowski, Charles. "face of a political candidate on a street billboard." Lines 1-5. *Play The Piano Drunk Like A Percussion Instrument Until The Fingers Begin To Bleed A Bit*. Santa Rosa, California: Black Sparrow Press, 2001. Page 77.

161. Bukowski, Charles. "Part 1." Lines 1-5. *Sifting Through The Madness For The Word, The Line, The Way: New Poems*. Edited by John Martin. New York: Harper Collins Publishers, 2003. Page 1.

162. Bukowski, Charles. ": : : the old movies." Lines 11-14. *The Days Run Away Like Wild Horses Over The Hills*. Santa Rosa, California: Black Sparrow Press, 2002. Page 33.

163. Bukowski, Charles. "days like razors, nights full of rats." Lines 1-2. *The Last Night of the Earth Poems*. Santa Rosa, California: Black Sparrow Press, 1992. Page 37.

164. Bukowski, Charles. "days like razors, nights full of rats." Lines 8-9. *The Last Night of the Earth Poems*. Santa Rosa, California: Black Sparrow Press, 1992. Page 37.

165. Bukowski, Charles. "work-fuck problems." Lines 45-46. *Sifting Through The Madness For The Word, The Line, The Way: New Poems*. Edited by John Martin. New York: Harper Collins Publishers, 2003. Page 92.

166. Bukowski, Charles. "love dead like a crushed fly." Lines 18-32. *The Night Torn Mad With Footsteps: New Poems*. New York: Harper Collins Publishers, 2003. Pages 58-59.

167. Bukowski, Charles. "Joe." Lines 73-74. *Slouching Toward Nirvana: New Poems*. Edited by John Martin. New York: Harper Collins Publishers, 2005. Page 261.

168. Bukowski, Charles. "mugged" Lines 14-22. *The Last Night of the Earth Poems*. Santa Rosa, California: Black Sparrow Press, 1992. Page 140.

169. Bukowski, Charles. "tonight." Lines 1-3. *Love is a Dog From Hell*. Santa Rosa, California: Black Sparrow Press, 2002. Page 36.

170. Bukowski, Charles. "john dillinger and *le chasseur maudit*." Lines 38-41. *Burning in Water Drowning in Flame*. Santa Barbara, California: Black Sparrow Press, 1985. Page 132.

171. Bukowski, Charles. "40 years ago." Lines 12-13. *The Night Torn Mad With Footsteps: New Poems*. New York: Harper Collins Publishers, 2003. Page 66.

172. Bukowski, Charles. "one to the breastplate." Lines 47-51. *Love is a Dog From Hell*. Santa Rosa, California: Black Sparrow Press, 2002. Page 118.

173. Bukowski, Charles. "meanwhile." Lines 12-16. *The Days Run Away Like Wild Horses Over The Hills*. Santa Rosa, California: Black Sparrow Press, 2002. Page 53.

174. Bukowski, Charles. "ice for the eagles." Lines 1-6. *The Days Run Away Like Wild Horses Over The Hills*. Santa Rosa, California: Black Sparrow Press, 2002. Page 30.

175. Bukowski, Charles. "john dillinger and *le chasseur maudit*." Lines 42-46. *Burning in Water Drowning in Flame*. Santa Barbara, California: Black Sparrow Press, 1985. Page 133.

176. Bukowski, Charles. "houses and dark streets." Lines 46-49. *Sifting Through The Madness For The Word, The Line, The Way: New Poems*. Edited by John Martin. New York: Harper Collins Publishers, 2003. Page 103.

177. Bukowski, Charles. "a strange day." Lines 1-5. *The Last Night of the Earth Poems*. Santa Rosa, California: Black Sparrow Press, 1992. Page 50.

178. Bukowski, Charles. "torched-out." Lines 181-184. *The Last Night of the Earth Poems*. Santa Rosa, California: Black Sparrow Press, 1992. Page 386.

179. Bukowski, Charles. "$1.25 a gallon." Lines 39-43. *The Flash of Lightning Behind The Mountain: New Poems*. Edited by John Martin. New York: Harper Collins Publishers, 2004. Page 48.

180. Bukowski, Charles. "view from the screen." Lines 14-15. *Burning in Water Drowning in Flame*. Santa Barbara, California: Black Sparrow Press, 1985. Page 51.

181. Bukowski, Charles. "part 1." Lines 1-3. *The Flash of Lightning Behind The Mountain: New Poems*. Edited by John Martin. New York: Harper Collins Publishers, 2004. Page 1.

182. Bukowski, Charles. "the stupidest thing I ever did." Lines 41-45. *Slouching Toward Nirvana: New Poems*. Edited by John Martin. New York: Harper Collins Publishers, 2005. Page 164.

183. Bukowski, Charles. "straight on." Lines 1-4. *Sifting Through The Madness For The Word, The Line, The Way: New Poems*. Edited by John Martin. New York: Harper Collins Publishers, 2003. Page 302.

184. Bukowski, Charles. "coupons" Lines 10-12. *Love is a Dog From Hell*. Santa Rosa, California: Black Sparrow Press, 2002. Page 121.

185. Bukowski, Charles. "a horse with greenblue eyes." Lines 10-14. *Love is a Dog From Hell*. Santa Rosa, California: Black Sparrow Press, 2002. Page 165.

186. Bukowski, Charles. "coming awake" Lines 10-14. *Sifting Through The Madness For The Word, The Line, The Way: New Poems*. Edited by John Martin. New York: Harper Collins Publishers, 2003. Page 332.

187. Bukowski, Charles. "the idiot." Lines 1-4. *The Last Night of the Earth Poems*. Santa Rosa, California: Black Sparrow Press, 1992. Page 346.

188. Bukowski, Charles. "the fish with yellow eyes and green fins leaps into the volcano." Lines 11-15. *The Night Torn Mad With Footsteps: New Poems*. New York: Harper Collins Publishers, 2003. Page 21.

189. Bukowski, Charles. "I have shitstains in my underwear too. " Lines 16-24. *Love is a Dog From Hell*. Santa Rosa, California: Black Sparrow Press, 2002. Page 209.

190. Bukowski, Charles. "liberty." Lines 1-8. *Love is a Dog From Hell*. Santa Rosa, California: Black Sparrow Press, 2002. Page 186.

191. Bukowski, Charles. "the fish with yellow eyes and green fins leaps into the volcano." Lines 31-34. *The Night Torn Mad With Footsteps: New Poems*. New York: Harper Collins Publishers, 2003. Page 22.

192. Bukowski, Charles. "a fine night." Lines 56-59. *Sifting Through The Madness For The Word, The Line, The Way: New Poems*. Edited by John Martin. New York: Harper Collins Publishers, 2003. Page 164.

193. Bukowski, Charles. "upon this time." Lines 12-16. *The Last Night of the Earth Poems*. Santa Rosa, California: Black Sparrow Press, 1992. Page 185.

194. Bukowski, Charles. "within the dense overcast." Lines 12-15. *The Last Night of the Earth Poems*. Santa Rosa, California: Black Sparrow Press, 1992. Page 361.

195. Bukowski, Charles. "in search of a hero." Lines 67-70. *Sifting Through The Madness For The Word, The Line, The Way: New Poems*. Edited by John Martin. New York: Harper Collins Publishers, 2003. Page 354.

196. Bukowski, Charles. "German." Lines 26-28. *The Flash of Lightning Behind The Mountain: New Poems*. Edited by John Martin. New York: Harper Collins Publishers, 2004. Page 3.

197. Bukowski, Charles. "on the continent." Lines 23-26. *Love is a Dog From Hell*. Santa Rosa, California: Black Sparrow Press, 2002. Page 146.

198. Bukowski, Charles. "the Greek." Lines 1-4. *Love is a Dog From Hell*. Santa Rosa, California: Black Sparrow Press, 2002. Page 237.

199. Bukowski, Charles. "yellow cab." Lines 15-19. *Love is a Dog From Hell*. Santa Rosa, California: Black Sparrow Press, 2002. Page 150.

200. Bukowski, Charles. "the bee." Lines 36-38. *Love is a Dog From Hell*. Santa Rosa, California: Black Sparrow Press, 2002. Page 215.

201. Bukowski, Charles. "you." Lines 1-3. *Love is a Dog From Hell*. Santa Rosa, California: Black Sparrow Press, 2002. Page 17.

202. Bukowski, Charles. "on the continent." Lines 3-10. *Love is a Dog From Hell*. Santa Rosa, California: Black Sparrow Press, 2002. Page 146.

203. Bukowski, Charles. "II." Lines 1-3. *The Days Run Away Like Wild Horses Over The Hills*. Santa Rosa, California: Black Sparrow Press, 2002. Page 59.

204. Bukowski, Charles. "there once was a woman who put her head into an oven." Lines 18-22. *Love is a Dog From Hell*. Santa Rosa, California: Black Sparrow Press, 2002. Page 131.

205. Bukowski, Charles. "the big lonely night." Lines 12-18. *Slouching Toward Nirvana: New Poems*. Edited by John Martin. New York: Harper Collins Publishers, 2005. Page 140.

206. Bukowski, Charles. "the big lonely night." Lines 20-22. *Slouching Toward Nirvana: New Poems*. Edited by John Martin. New York: Harper Collins Publishers, 2005. Page 140.

207. Bukowski, Charles. "in search of a hero." Lines 158-161. *Sifting Through The Madness For The Word, The Line, The Way: New Poems*. Edited by John Martin. New York: Harper Collins Publishers, 2003. Page 357.

208. Bukowski, Charles. "untitled." Lines 1-3. *Burning in Water Drowning in Flame*. Santa Barbara, California: Black Sparrow Press, 1985. Page 50.

209. Bukowski, Charles. "leaning on wood." Lines 45-47. *Play The Piano Drunk Like A Percussion Instrument Until The Fingers Begin To Bleed A Bit*. Santa Rosa, California: Black Sparrow Press, 2001. Page 19.

210. Bukowski, Charles. "a poem is a city." Lines 1-9. *The Days Run Away Like Wild Horses Over The Hills*. Santa Rosa, California: Black Sparrow Press, 2002. Page 54.

211. Bukowski, Charles. "my Uncle Jack." Lines 1-27. *The Last Night of the Earth Poems*. Santa Rosa, California: Black Sparrow Press, 1992. Page 330.

212. Bukowski, Charles. "a lady who wants to help?" Lines 13-16. *The Night Torn Mad With Footsteps: New Poems*. New York: Harper Collins Publishers, 2003. Page 33.

213. Bukowski, Charles. "words for you." Lines 6-10. *Sifting Through The Madness For The Word, The Line, The Way: New Poems*. Edited by John Martin. New York: Harper Collins Publishers, 2003. Page 296.

214. Bukowski, Charles. "vulgar poem." Lines 4-9. *Slouching Toward Nirvana: New Poems*. Edited by John Martin. New York: Harper Collins Publishers, 2005. Page 128.

215. Bukowski, Charles. "vulgar poem." Lines 97-100. *Slouching Toward Nirvana: New Poems*. Edited by John Martin. New York: Harper Collins Publishers, 2005. Page 131.

216. Bukowski, Charles. "what a writer." Lines 1-4. *The Last Night of the Earth Poems*. Santa Rosa, California: Black Sparrow Press, 1992. Page 337.

217. Bukowski, Charles. "the word." Lines 15-18. *The Last Night of the Earth Poems*. Santa Rosa, California: Black Sparrow Press, 1992. Page 387.

218. Bukowski, Charles. "it's strange." Lines 27-30. *Slouching Toward Nirvana: New Poems*. Edited by John Martin. New York: Harper Collins Publishers, 2005. Page 265.

219. Bukowski, Charles. "interviews." Lines 51-54. *Play The Piano Drunk Like A Percussion Instrument Until The Fingers Begin To Bleed A Bit*. Santa Rosa, California: Black Sparrow Press, 2001. Page 76.

220. Bukowski, Charles. "the poetry game." Lines 1-8. *The Flash of Lightning Behind The Mountain: New Poems*. Edited by John Martin. New York: Harper Collins Publishers, 2004. Page 91.

221. Bukowski, Charles. "the happy life of the tired." Lines 3-6. *Play The Piano Drunk Like A Percussion Instrument Until The Fingers Begin To Bleed A Bit*. Santa Rosa, California: Black Sparrow Press, 2001. Page 96.

222. Bukowski, Charles. "the word." Lines 26-29. *The Last Night of the Earth Poems*. Santa Rosa, California: Black Sparrow Press, 1992. Page 387.

223. Bukowski, Charles. "zero." Lines 15-19. *The Last Night of the Earth Poems*. Santa Rosa, California: Black Sparrow Press, 1992. Page 179.

224. Bukowski, Charles. "the word." Lines 112-116. *The Last Night of the Earth Poems*. Santa Rosa, California: Black Sparrow Press, 1992. Page 390.

225. Bukowski, Charles. "the interview." Lines 39-44. *Sifting Through The Madness For The Word, The Line, The Way: New Poems*. Edited by John Martin. New York: Harper Collins Publishers, 2003. Page 139.

226. Bukowski, Charles. "betrayed." Lines 14-18. *The Last Night of the Earth Poems*. Santa Rosa, California: Black Sparrow Press, 1992. Page 380.

227. Bukowski, Charles. "regrets of a sort." Lines 60-67. *Sifting Through The Madness For The Word, The Line, The Way: New Poems*. Edited by John Martin. New York: Harper Collins Publishers, 2003. Page 370.

228. Bukowski, Charles. "I'm flattered." Lines 36-39. *Sifting Through The Madness For The Word, The Line, The Way: New Poems*. Edited by John Martin. New York: Harper Collins Publishers, 2003. Page 130.

229. Bukowski, Charles. "sloppy day." Lines 1-4. *Sifting Through The Madness For The Word, The Line, The Way: New Poems*. Edited by John Martin. New York: Harper Collins Publishers, 2003. Page 317.

230. Bukowski, Charles. "my comrades." Lines 35-38. *Love is a Dog From Hell*. Santa Rosa, California: Black Sparrow Press, 2002. Page 240.

231. Bukowski, Charles. "trench warfare." Lines 70-74. *Love is a Dog From Hell*. Santa Rosa, California: Black Sparrow Press, 2002. Page 126.

232. Bukowski, Charles. "my German buddy." Lines 5-6. *The Last Night of the Earth Poems*. Santa Rosa, California: Black Sparrow Press, 1992. Page 22.

233. Bukowski, Charles. "classical music and me." Lines 70-71. *The Last Night of the Earth Poems*. Santa Rosa, California: Black Sparrow Press, 1992. Page 372.

234. Bukowski, Charles. "Bonaparte's Retreat." Lines 37-42. *The Last Night of the Earth Poems*. Santa Rosa, California: Black Sparrow Press, 1992. Page 296.

235. Bukowski, Charles. "A.D. 701-762." Lines 1-13. *Sifting Through The Madness For The Word, The Line, The Way: New Poems*. Edited by John Martin. New York: Harper Collins Publishers, 2003. Page 366.

236. Bukowski, Charles. "notations." Lines 25-27. *The Flash of Lightning Behind The Mountain: New Poems*. Edited by John Martin. New York: Harper Collins Publishers, 2004. Page 230.

237. Bukowski, Charles. "war some of the time." Lines 1-2. *Sifting Through The Madness For The Word, The Line, The Way: New Poems*. Edited by John Martin. New York: Harper Collins Publishers, 2003. Page 382.

238. Bukowski, Charles. "a lovely couple." Lines 1-4. *Love is a Dog From Hell*. Santa Rosa, California: Black Sparrow Press, 2002. Page 223.

239. Bukowski, Charles. "99 to one." Lines 17-20. *Love is a Dog From Hell*. Santa Rosa, California: Black Sparrow Press, 2002. Page 160.

240. Bukowski, Charles. "my groupie." Lines 17-21. *Love is a Dog From Hell*. Santa Rosa, California: Black Sparrow Press, 2002. Page 231.

241. Bukowski, Charles. ": : : the days run away like wild horses over the hill." Lines 135-137. *The Days Run Away Like Wild Horses Over The Hills*. Santa Rosa, California: Black Sparrow Press, 2002. Page 156.

242. Bukowski, Charles. "as crazy as I ever was" Lines 13-15. *Love is a Dog From Hell*. Santa Rosa, California: Black Sparrow Press, 2002. Page 252.

243. Bukowski, Charles. "Trollius and trellises." Lines 84-91. *The Last Night of the Earth Poems*. Santa Rosa, California: Black Sparrow Press, 1992. Page 56.

244. Bukowski, Charles. "a poet in New York." Lines 1-9. *The Last Night of the Earth Poems*. Santa Rosa, California: Black Sparrow Press, 1992. Page 130.

245. Bukowski, Charles. "artist." Lines 9-12. *Love is a Dog From Hell*. Santa Rosa, California: Black Sparrow Press, 2002. Page 290.

246. Sebestyen, Marta. "Szerelem, Szerelem (Love, Love)" This song was made popular by the film "The English Patient."

247. Bukowski, Charles. "now, Ezra,." Line 35. *Slouching Toward Nirvana: New Poems.* Edited by John Martin. New York: Harper Collins Publishers, 2005. Page 188.

248. Bukowski, Charles. "poetry" Lines 1-13. *The Last Night of the Earth Poems.* Santa Rosa, California: Black Sparrow Press, 1992. Page 94.

249. Bukowski, Charles. "writing." Lines 34-36. *The Flash of Lightning Behind The Mountain: New Poems.* Edited by John Martin. New York: Harper Collins Publishers, 2004. Page 226.

ALLEN GINSBERG SECTION

250. Ginsberg, Allen. *America. The Norton Anthology of Modern Poetry: Second Edition.* Lines 1-13. Edited by Richard Ellmann and Robert O'Clair. New York: W.W. Norton & Company, 1985. Page 1216. (For the sake of brevity, I have only excerpted the opening 13 lines from Ginsberg's poem, but I would recommend to the reader to read the entire poem, as doing so, adds both perspective and context to my riposte.)

251. The refrain from Beck's 1993 popular song 'Loser.'

FRANK O'HARA SECTION

252. O'Hara, Frank. "LES LUTHS." Lines 4-5. *The Collected Poems of Frank O'Hara.* Edited by Donald Allen. Introduction by John Ashbery. Los Angeles: University of California Press, 1995. Page 343.

253. O'Hara, Frank. "TO RICHARD MILLER." Lines 1-6. *The Collected Poems of Frank O'Hara.* Edited by Donald Allen. Introduction by John Ashbery. Los Angeles: University of California Press, 1995. Page 301.

254. O'Hara, Frank. "STEPS." Lines 16-20. *The Collected Poems of Frank O'Hara.* Edited by Donald Allen. Introduction by John Ashbery. Los Angeles: University of California Press, 1995. Page 371.

255. O'Hara, Frank. "FOUR LITTLE ELEGIES." Lines 32-38. *The Collected Poems of Frank O'Hara.* Edited by Donald Allen. Introduction by John Ashbery. Los Angeles: University of California Press, 1995. Page 248.

256. O'Hara, Frank. "FOUR LITTLE ELEGIES." Lines 1-9. *The Collected Poems of Frank O'Hara.* Edited by Donald Allen. Introduction by John Ashbery. Los Angeles: University of California Press, 1995. Page 248.

257. O'Hara, Frank. "BILL'S BURNOOSE." Lines 30-32. *The Collected Poems of Frank O'Hara.* Edited by Donald Allen. Introduction by John Ashbery. Los Angeles: University of California Press, 1995. Page 416.

258. O'Hara, Frank. "FOR THE CHINESE NEW YEAR & FOR BILL BERKSON." Lines 81-85. *The Collected Poems of Frank O'Hara.* Edited by Donald Allen. Introduction by John Ashbery. Los Angeles: University of California Press, 1995. Page 391.

259. O'Hara, Frank. "A STEP AWAY FROM THEM." Lines 34-38. *The Collected Poems of Frank O'Hara.* Edited by Donald Allen. Introduction by John Ashbery. Los Angeles: University of California Press, 1995. Page 258.

260. O'Hara, Frank. "ODE ON CAUSALITY." Lines 8-11. *The Collected Poems of Frank O'Hara.* Edited by Donald Allen. Introduction by John Ashbery. Los Angeles: University of California Press, 1995. Page 302.

261. O'Hara, Frank. "HISTORICAL VARIATIONS." Lines 11-12. *The Collected Poems of Frank O'Hara.* Edited by Donald Allen. Introduction by John Ashbery. Los Angeles: University of California Press, 1995. Page 490.

262. O'Hara, Frank. "HAVING A COKE WITH YOU." Lines 17-18. *The Collected Poems of Frank O'Hara.* Edited by Donald Allen. Introduction by John Ashbery. Los Angeles: University of California Press, 1995. Page 360.

263. O'Hara, Frank. "MAUNDY SATURDAY." Line 1. *The Collected Poems of Frank O'Hara.* Edited by Donald Allen. Introduction by John Ashbery. Los Angeles: University of California Press, 1995. Page 455.

264. O'Hara, Frank. "POEM." Lines 13-16. *The Collected Poems of Frank O'Hara.* Edited by Donald Allen. Introduction by John Ashbery. Los Angeles: University of California Press, 1995. Page 477.

265. O'Hara, Frank. "THE "UNFINISHED" *In Memory of Bunny Lang.*" Lines 40-43. *Frank O'Hara Selected Poems.* Edited by Mark Ford. New York: Alfred A. Knopf, 2008. Page 153.

266. O'Hara, Frank. "ODE TO MICHAEL GOLDBERG ('S BIRTH AND OTHER BIRTHS." Lines 75-77. *The Collected Poems of Frank O'Hara.* Edited by Donald Allen. Introduction by John Ashbery. Los Angeles: University of California Press, 1995. Page 292.

267. O'Hara, Frank. "ON RACHMANINOFF'S BIRTHDAY & ABOUT ARSHILE GORKY." Lines 19-20. *The Collected Poems of Frank O'Hara.* Edited by Donald Allen. Introduction by John Ashbery. Los Angeles: University of California Press, 1995. Page 474.

268. Helprin, Mark. *Against the Dehumanization of Art.* The New Criterion. September, 1994. Pages 91-94.

269. O'Hara, Frank. "RADIO." Lines 13-15. *The Collected Poems of Frank O'Hara.* Edited by Donald Allen. Introduction by John Ashbery. Los Angeles: University of California Press, 1995. Page 234.

270. O'Hara, Frank. "BILL'S SCHOOL OF NEW YORK." Lines 5-8. *The Collected Poems of Frank O'Hara.* Edited by Donald Allen. Introduction by John Ashbery. Los Angeles: University of California Press, 1995. Page 415.

271. O'Hara, Frank. "AT JOAN'S." Lines 6-10. *The Collected Poems of Frank O'Hara.* Edited by Donald Allen. Introduction by John Ashbery. Los Angeles: University of California Press, 1995. Page 327.

272. O'Hara, Frank. "ON RACMANINOFF'S BIRTHDAY." Lines 1-5. *Frank O'Hara Selected Poems.* Edited by Mark Ford. New York: Alfred A. Knopf, 2008. Page 64.

273. O'Hara, Frank. "VARIATIONS ON THE "TREE OF HEAVEN."" Lines 1-5. *The Collected Poems of Frank O'Hara.* Edited by Donald Allen. Introduction by John Ashbery. Los Angeles: University of California Press, 1995. Page 349.

274. O'Hara, Frank. "SECOND AVENUE." Lines 410-412. *The Collected Poems of Frank O'Hara.* Edited by Donald Allen. Introduction by John Ashbery. Los Angeles: University of California Press, 1995. Pages 148-149.

275. O'Hara, Frank. "[NOTES ON SECOND AVENUE]." Lines 73-84. *The Collected Poems of Frank O'Hara.* Edited by Donald Allen. Introduction by John Ashbery. Los Angeles: University of California Press, 1995. Page 497.

276. O'Hara, Frank. "MEMORIAL DAY 1950." Line 1. *The Collected Poems of Frank O'Hara.* Edited by Donald Allen. Introduction by John Ashbery. Los Angeles: University of California Press, 1995. Page 17.

277. O'Hara, Frank. ""L'AMOUR AVAIT PASSE PAR LA."" Lines 26-27. *The Collected Poems of Frank O'Hara.* Edited by Donald Allen. Introduction by John Ashbery. Los Angeles: University of California Press, 1995. Page 333.

278. O'Hara, Frank. "LARRY RIVERS: A MEMOIR." Lines 34-35. *The Collected Poems of Frank O'Hara.* Edited by Donald Allen. Introduction by John Ashbery. Los Angeles: University of California Press, 1995. Page 512.

279. O'Hara, Frank. "A TERRESTRIAL CUCKOO." Lines 44-45. *The Collected Poems of Frank O'Hara.* Edited by Donald Allen. Introduction by John Ashbery. Los Angeles: University of California Press, 1995. Page 63.

280. O'Hara, Frank. "FAVORITE PAINTING IN THE METROPOLITAN." Lines 19-22. *The Collected Poems of Frank O'Hara.* Edited by Donald Allen. Introduction by John Ashbery. Los Angeles: University of California Press, 1995. Page 423.

281. O'Hara, Frank. "DIGRESSION ON NUMBER 1, 1948." Lines 13-17. *The Collected Poems of Frank O'Hara.* Edited by Donald Allen. Introduction by John Ashbery. Los Angeles: University of California Press, 1995. Page 260.

282. O'Hara, Frank. "DIGRESSION ON NUMBER 1, 1948." Lines 5-10. *The Collected Poems of Frank O'Hara*. Edited by Donald Allen. Introduction by John Ashbery. Los Angeles: University of California Press, 1995. Page 260.

283. O'Hara, Frank. "SECOND AVENUE." Lines 135-136. *The Collected Poems of Frank O'Hara*. Edited by Donald Allen. Introduction by John Ashbery. Los Angeles: University of California Press, 1995. Page 142.

284. O'Hara, Frank. "LINES FOR THE FORTUNE COOKIES." Line 23. *The Collected Poems of Frank O'Hara*. Edited by Donald Allen. Introduction by John Ashbery. Los Angeles: University of California Press, 1995. Page 466.

285. O'Hara, Frank. "MEMORIAL DAY 1950." Lines 14-22. *Frank O'Hara Selected Poems*. Edited by Mark Ford. New York: Alfred A. Knopf, 2008. Page 7.

286. O'Hara, Frank. "POEM." Lines 28-31. *The Collected Poems of Frank O'Hara*. Edited by Donald Allen. Introduction by John Ashbery. Los Angeles: University of California Press, 1995. Page 340.

287. O'Hara, Frank. "MEDITATIONS IN AN EMERGENCY." Lines 28-29. *The Collected Poems of Frank O'Hara*. Edited by Donald Allen. Introduction by John Ashbery. Los Angeles: University of California Press, 1995. Page 197.

288. O'Hara, Frank. "TO A POET." Lines 7-11. *The Collected Poems of Frank O'Hara*. Edited by Donald Allen. Introduction by John Ashbery. Los Angeles: University of California Press, 1995. Page 185.

289. O'Hara, Frank. "[THE LIGHT PRESSES DOWN]." Lines 24-27. *The Collected Poems of Frank O'Hara*. Edited by Donald Allen. Introduction by John Ashbery. Los Angeles: University of California Press, 1995. Page 476.

290. O'Hara, Frank. "POEM." Lines 13-14. *The Collected Poems of Frank O'Hara*. Edited by Donald Allen. Introduction by John Ashbery. Los Angeles: University of California Press, 1995. Page 340.

291. O'Hara, Frank. "3 POEMS ABOUT KENNETH KOCH." Line 6. *The Collected Poems of Frank O'Hara*. Edited by Donald Allen. Introduction by John Ashbery. Los Angeles: University of California Press, 1995. Page 151.

292. O'Hara, Frank. "FAILURES OF SPRING." Lines 1-2. *The Collected Poems of Frank O'Hara*. Edited by Donald Allen. Introduction by John Ashbery. Los Angeles: University of California Press, 1995. Page 274.

293. O'Hara, Frank. "POEM." Lines 1-2. *The Collected Poems of Frank O'Hara*. Edited by Donald Allen. Introduction by John Ashbery. Los Angeles: University of California Press, 1995. Page 334.

294. O'Hara, Frank. "JOE'S JACKET." Line 26. *The Collected Poems of Frank O'Hara*. Edited by Donald Allen. Introduction by John Ashbery. Los Angeles: University of California Press, 1995. Page 330.

295. O'Hara, Frank. "LARRY RIVERS: A MEMOIR." Lines 58-59. *The Collected Poems of Frank O'Hara*. Edited by Donald Allen. Introduction by John Ashbery. Los Angeles: University of California Press, 1995. Page 513.

296. O'Hara, Frank. "POEM READ AT JOAN MITCHELL'S." Lines 21-25. *The Collected Poems of Frank O'Hara*. Edited by Donald Allen. Introduction by John Ashbery. Los Angeles: University of California Press, 1995. Page 265.

297. O'Hara, Frank. "NIGHT THOUGHTS IN GREENWICH VILLAGE." Lines 22-25. *The Collected Poems of Frank O'Hara*. Edited by Donald Allen. Introduction by John Ashbery. Los Angeles: University of California Press, 1995. Page 38.

298. O'Hara, Frank. "DIALOGUES." Lines 20. *The Collected Poems of Frank O'Hara*. Edited by Donald Allen. Introduction by John Ashbery. Los Angeles: University of California Press, 1995. Page 241.

299. O'Hara, Frank. "NIGHT THOUGHTS IN GREENWICH VILLAGE." Lines 1-2. *The Collected Poems of Frank O'Hara*. Edited by Donald Allen. Introduction by John Ashbery. Los Angeles: University of California Press, 1995. Page 38.

300. O'Hara, Frank. "FANTASY." Lines 20-23. *The Collected Poems of Frank O'Hara.* Edited by Donald Allen. Introduction by John Ashbery. Los Angeles: University of California Press, 1995. Page 488.

301. O'Hara, Frank. "BIOGRAPHIA LETTERARIA." Lines 11-28. *The Collected Poems of Frank O'Hara.* Edited by Donald Allen. Introduction by John Ashbery. Los Angeles: University of California Press, 1995. Page 464.

302. Pirinaca, Tia Anica la. "GYPSY CANTE." Line 1. *GYPSY CANTE: deep song of the caves.* Translated by Will Kirkland. San Francisco: City Light Books, 1999. Page xv.

303. O'Hara, Frank. "PERSONISM: A MANIFESTO." Lines 5-6. *The Collected Poems of Frank O'Hara.* Edited by Donald Allen. Introduction by John Ashbery. Los Angeles: University of California Press, 1995. Page 498.

304. O'Hara, Frank. "Larry Rivers: A Memoir." Lines 40-41. *Frank O'Hara Selected Poems.* Edited by Mark Ford. New York: Alfred A. Knopf, 2008. Page 256

305. O'Hara, Frank. "Larry Rivers: A Memoir." Lines 21-24. *Frank O'Hara Selected Poems.* Edited by Mark Ford. New York: Alfred A. Knopf, 2008. Page 255.

306. O'Hara Frank. "Teens Quiz A Critic: "What's With Modern Art?"" *WHAT'S WITH MODERN ART?: Selected Short Reviews & Other Art Writings.* Edited by Bill Berkson. Austin, Texas: Mike & Dale's Press, 1999. Page 29.

307. O'Hara, Frank. "NAPTHA." Lines 40-42. *Frank O'Hara Selected Poems.* Edited by Mark Ford. New York: Alfred A. Knopf, 2008. Page 173.

308. O'Hara, Frank. "ODE TO WILLEM DE KOONING." Lines 59-61. *Frank O'Hara Selected Poems.* Edited by Mark Ford. New York: Alfred A. Knopf, 2008. Page 127.

309. O'Hara, Frank. "ODE TO WILLEM DE KOONING." Lines 62-63. *Frank O'Hara Selected Poems.* Edited by Mark Ford. New York: Alfred A. Knopf, 2008. Page 127.

310. O'Hara, Frank. "ODE TO WILLEM DE KOONING." Lines 64-67. *Frank O'Hara Selected Poems.* Edited by Mark Ford. New York: Alfred A. Knopf, 2008. Page 128.

311. O'Hara, Frank. "1951." Lines 1-2. *The Collected Poems of Frank O'Hara.* Edited by Donald Allen. Introduction by John Ashbery. Los Angeles: University of California Press, 1995. Page 73.

312. O'Hara, Frank. "I LOVE THE WAY IT GOES." Lines 7-9. *The Collected Poems of Frank O'Hara.* Edited by Donald Allen. Introduction by John Ashbery. Los Angeles: University of California Press, 1995. Page 481.

313. O'Hara, Frank. "SONNET." Line 12. *The Collected Poems of Frank O'Hara.* Edited by Donald Allen. Introduction by John Ashbery. Los Angeles: University of California Press, 1995. Page 131.

314. O'Hara, Frank. "TWO VARIATIONS." Lines 1-3. *The Collected Poems of Frank O'Hara.* Edited by Donald Allen. Introduction by John Ashbery. Los Angeles: University of California Press, 1995. Page 134.

315. O'Hara, Frank. "GRAND CENTRAL." Lines 13-16. *The Collected Poems of Frank O'Hara.* Edited by Donald Allen. Introduction by John Ashbery. Los Angeles: University of California Press, 1995. Page 168.

316. O'Hara, Frank. "TO JANE, SOME AIR." Lines 1-2. *The Collected Poems of Frank O'Hara.* Edited by Donald Allen. Introduction by John Ashbery. Los Angeles: University of California Press, 1995. Page 192.

317. O'Hara, Frank. "TO JANE, SOME AIR." Lines 12-13. *The Collected Poems of Frank O'Hara.* Edited by Donald Allen. Introduction by John Ashbery. Los Angeles: University of California Press, 1995. Page 192.

318. O'Hara, Frank. "LIFE ON EARTH." Line 39. *The Collected Poems of Frank O'Hara.* Edited by Donald Allen. Introduction by John Ashbery. Los Angeles: University of California Press, 1995. Page 156.

319. O'Hara, Frank. "VARIATIONS ON SATURDAY." Lines 60-61. *The Collected Poems of Frank O'Hara*. Edited by Donald Allen. Introduction by John Ashbery. Los Angeles: University of California Press, 1995. Page 378.

320. O'Hara, Frank. "SNEDEN'S LANDING VARIATIONS." Lines 33-36. *The Collected Poems of Frank O'Hara*. Edited by Donald Allen. Introduction by John Ashbery. Los Angeles: University of California Press, 1995. Page 162.

321. O'Hara, Frank. "SONG." Lines 1-3. *The Collected Poems of Frank O'Hara*. Edited by Donald Allen. Introduction by John Ashbery. Los Angeles: University of California Press, 1995. Page 361.

322. O'Hara, Frank. "JOHN BUTTON BIRTHDAY." Lines 37-39. *The Collected Poems of Frank O'Hara*. Edited by Donald Allen. Introduction by John Ashbery. Los Angeles: University of California Press, 1995. Page 268.

323. O'Hara, Frank. "A WARM DAY FOR DECEMBER." Lines 1-9. *The Collected Poems of Frank O'Hara*. Edited by Donald Allen. Introduction by John Ashbery. Los Angeles: University of California Press, 1995. Pages 375-376.

324. O'Hara, Frank. "AT JOAN'S." Lines 6-10. *The Collected Poems of Frank O'Hara*. Edited by Donald Allen. Introduction by John Ashbery. Los Angeles: University of California Press, 1995. Page 327.

325. O'Hara, Frank. "GALANTA." Lines 13-15. *The Collected Poems of Frank O'Hara*. Edited by Donald Allen. Introduction by John Ashbery. Los Angeles: University of California Press, 1995. Page 463.

326. O'Hara, Frank. "POEM." Lines 1-13. *The Collected Poems of Frank O'Hara*. Edited by Donald Allen. Introduction by John Ashbery. Los Angeles: University of California Press, 1995. Page 449.

327. O'Hara, Frank. "AGGRESSION." Lines 22-25. *The Collected Poems of Frank O'Hara*. Edited by Donald Allen. Introduction by John Ashbery. Los Angeles: University of California Press, 1995. Page 264.

328. O'Hara, Frank. "YESTERDAY DOWN AT THE CANAL." Line 2. *The Collected Poems of Frank O'Hara*. Edited by Donald Allen. Introduction by John Ashbery. Los Angeles: University of California Press, 1995. Page 429.

329. O'Hara, Frank. "ON RACHMANINOFF'S BIRTHDAY #158." Lines 16-18. *The Collected Poems of Frank O'Hara*. Edited by Donald Allen. Introduction by John Ashbery. Los Angeles: University of California Press, 1995. Page 418.

330. O'Hara, Frank. "AT JOAN'S." Lines 1-5. *The Collected Poems of Frank O'Hara*. Edited by Donald Allen. Introduction by John Ashbery. Los Angeles: University of California Press, 1995. Page 327.

331. O'Hara, Frank. "POEM." Lines 16-17. *The Collected Poems of Frank O'Hara*. Edited by Donald Allen. Introduction by John Ashbery. Los Angeles: University of California Press, 1995. Page 215.

332. O'Hara, Frank. "ST. PAUL AND ALL THAT." Lines 33-34. *The Collected Poems of Frank O'Hara*. Edited by Donald Allen. Introduction by John Ashbery. Los Angeles: University of California Press, 1995. Page 407.

333. O'Hara, Frank. "ADIEU TO NORMAN, BON JOUR TO JOAN AND JEAN-PAUL." Lines 1-2. *The Collected Poems of Frank O'Hara*. Edited by Donald Allen. Introduction by John Ashbery. Los Angeles: University of California Press, 1995. Page 328.

334. O'Hara, Frank. "THE DAY LADY DIED." Lines 1-6. *The Collected Poems of Frank O'Hara*. Edited by Donald Allen. Introduction by John Ashbery. Los Angeles: University of California Press, 1995. Page 325.

335. O'Hara, Frank. "ANN ARBOR VARIATIONS: 4." Lines 62-65. *The Collected Poems of Frank O'Hara*. Edited by Donald Allen. Introduction by John Ashbery. Los Angeles: University of California Press, 1995. Page 66.

336. O'Hara, Frank. "MY HEART." Lines 11-12. *The Collected Poems of Frank O'Hara*. Edited by Donald Allen. Introduction by John Ashbery. Los Angeles: University of California Press, 1995. Page 231.

337. O'Hara, Frank. "STEPS." Lines 1-3. *The Collected Poems of Frank O'Hara*. Edited by Donald Allen. Introduction by John Ashbery. Los Angeles: University of California Press, 1995. Page 370.

338. O'Hara, Frank. "CROW HILL." Lines 31-33. *The Collected Poems of Frank O'Hara*. Edited by Donald Allen. Introduction by John Ashbery. Los Angeles: University of California Press, 1995. Page 348.

339. O'Hara, Frank. "MEDITATIONS IN AN EMERGENCY." Lines 11-12. *The Collected Poems of Frank O'Hara*. Edited by Donald Allen. Introduction by John Ashbery. Los Angeles: University of California Press, 1995. Page 197.

340. O'Hara, Frank. "A STEP AWAY FROM THEM." Lines 15-17. *The Collected Poems of Frank O'Hara*. Edited by Donald Allen. Introduction by John Ashbery. Los Angeles: University of California Press, 1995. Page 257.

341. O'Hara, Frank. "F.MI. 6/25/61." Line 40. *The Collected Poems of Frank O'Hara*. Edited by Donald Allen. Introduction by John Ashbery. Los Angeles: University of California Press, 1995. Page 411.

342. O'Hara, Frank. "POEM READ AT JOAN MITCHELL'S." Lines 17-18. *The Collected Poems of Frank O'Hara*. Edited by Donald Allen. Introduction by John Ashbery. Los Angeles: University of California Press, 1995. Page 265.

343. O'Hara, Frank. "A WARM DAY FOR DECEMBER." Lines 25-28. *The Collected Poems of Frank O'Hara*. Edited by Donald Allen. Introduction by John Ashbery. Los Angeles: University of California Press, 1995. Page 376.

344. O'Hara, Frank. "RHAPSODY." Lines 1-2. *The Collected Poems of Frank O'Hara*. Edited by Donald Allen. Introduction by John Ashbery. Los Angeles: University of California Press, 1995. Page 325.

345. O'Hara, Frank. "F. (MISSIVE & WALK) I. #53" Lines 17-19. *Frank O'Hara Selected Poems*. Edited by Mark Ford. New York: Alfred A. Knopf, 2008. Page 215.

346. O'Hara, Frank. "NOW THAT I AM IN MADRID AND CAN THINK." Line 5. *The Collected Poems of Frank O'Hara*. Edited by Donald Allen. Introduction by John Ashbery. Los Angeles: University of California Press, 1995. Page 356.

347. O'Hara, Frank. "THE "UNFINISHED."" Lines 63-65. *The Collected Poems of Frank O'Hara*. Edited by Donald Allen. Introduction by John Ashbery. Los Angeles: University of California Press, 1995. Page 318.

348. O'Hara, Frank. "HOTEL PARTICULIER." Lines 1-3. *The Collected Poems of Frank O'Hara*. Edited by Donald Allen. Introduction by John Ashbery. Los Angeles: University of California Press, 1995. Page 359.

349. O'Hara, Frank. "WITH BARBARA AT LARRE'S" Lines 8-9. *The Collected Poems of Frank O'Hara*. Edited by Donald Allen. Introduction by John Ashbery. Los Angeles: University of California Press, 1995. Page 227.

350. Excerpted from Giacomo Puccini's *Tosca*. The line, 'Is your blood choking you?' is uttered by Tosca to Scarpia at the denouement of Act II after she fatally stabs him.

351. O'Hara, Frank. "SONG." Lines 1-20. *Frank O'Hara Selected Poems*. Edited by Mark Ford. New York: Alfred A. Knopf, 2008. Page 19.

352. O'Hara, Frank. "POEM READ AT JOAN MITCHELL'S." Line 10. *The Collected Poems of Frank O'Hara*. Edited by Donald Allen. Introduction by John Ashbery. Los Angeles: University of California Press, 1995. Page 265.

353. O'Hara, Frank. "3 POEMS ABOUT KENNETH KOCH." Line 35-36. *The Collected Poems of Frank O'Hara*. Edited by Donald Allen. Introduction by John Ashbery. Los Angeles: University of California Press, 1995. Page 152.

354. O'Hara, Frank. "SECOND AVENUE." Lines 367-368. *The Collected Poems of Frank O'Hara*. Edited by Donald Allen. Introduction by John Ashbery. Los Angeles: University of California Press, 1995. Page 148.

355. O'Hara, Frank. "LES LUTHS." Line 1. *The Collected Poems of Frank O'Hara*. Edited by Donald Allen. Introduction by John Ashbery. Los Angeles: University of California Press, 1995. Page 343.

356. O'Hara, Frank. "THE OLD MACHINIST." Line 26. *The Collected Poems of Frank O'Hara*. Edited by Donald Allen. Introduction by John Ashbery. Los Angeles: University of California Press, 1995. Page 457.

357. O'Hara, Frank. "[THE SAD THING ABOUT LIFE IS]." Lines 1-6. *The Collected Poems of Frank O'Hara*. Edited by Donald Allen. Introduction by John Ashbery. Los Angeles: University of California Press, 1995. Page 323.

358. O'Hara, Frank. "MEDITATIONS IN AN EMERGENCY." Line 17. *The Collected Poems of Frank O'Hara*. Edited by Donald Allen. Introduction by John Ashbery. Los Angeles: University of California Press, 1995. Page 197.

359. O'Hara, Frank. "PERSONISM: A MANIFESTO." Lines 49-51. *The Collected Poems of Frank O'Hara*. Edited by Donald Allen. Introduction by John Ashbery. Los Angeles: University of California Press, 1995. Page 499.

360. O'Hara, Frank. "ABOUT COURBET." Lines 64-65. *The Collected Poems of Frank O'Hara*. Edited by Donald Allen. Introduction by John Ashbery. Los Angeles: University of California Press, 1995. Page 288.

361. O'Hara, Frank. "EASTER." Lines 127-128. *The Collected Poems of Frank O'Hara*. Edited by Donald Allen. Introduction by John Ashbery. Los Angeles: University of California Press, 1995. Page 99.

362. O'Hara, Frank. "TO THE MOUNTAINS IN NEW YORK." Lines 39-41. *The Collected Poems of Frank O'Hara*. Edited by Donald Allen. Introduction by John Ashbery. Los Angeles: University of California Press, 1995. Page 199.

363. O'Hara, Frank. "TO THE MOUNTAINS IN NEW YORK." Lines 25-32. *Frank O'Hara Selected Poems*. Edited by Mark Ford. New York: Alfred A. Knopf, 2008. Page 68.

364. O'Hara, Frank. "IN MEMORY OF MY FEELINGS." Lines 81-86. *The Collected Poems of Frank O'Hara*. Edited by Donald Allen. Introduction by John Ashbery. Los Angeles: University of California Press, 1995. Page 254.

365. 'Habibi ya nour il ain' is translated from Arabic as 'My dear, you are the light of my eyes' and is the title of a popular song by Amr Diab.

366. Spoken by Faisal Shahzad in taped video statement prior to his failed Times Square Bombing. http://www.youtube.com/watch?v=hwOiXxTOxrA

367. O'Hara, Frank. "MEDITATIONS IN AN EMERGENCY." Line 1. *The Collected Poems of Frank O'Hara*. Edited by Donald Allen. Introduction by John Ashbery. Los Angeles: University of California Press, 1995. Page 197.

368. O'Hara, Frank. "LIFE ON EARTH." Lines 91-97. *The Collected Poems of Frank O'Hara*. Edited by Donald Allen. Introduction by John Ashbery. Los Angeles: University of California Press, 1995. Page 157.

369. O'Hara, Frank. "THE THREE-PENNY OPERA." Lines 24-27. *The Collected Poems of Frank O'Hara*. Edited by Donald Allen. Introduction by John Ashbery. Los Angeles: University of California Press, 1995. Page 32.

370. O'Hara, Frank. "OCTOBER." Lines 25-32. *Frank O'Hara Selected Poems*. Edited by Mark Ford. New York: Alfred A. Knopf, 2008. Page 32.

371. O'Hara, Frank. "STEPS." Lines 41-45. *The Collected Poems of Frank O'Hara*. Edited by Donald Allen. Introduction by John Ashbery. Los Angeles: University of California Press, 1995. Page 371.

372. O'Hara, Frank. "MEDITATIONS IN AN EMERGENCY." Line 7. *The Collected Poems of Frank O'Hara*. Edited by Donald Allen. Introduction by John Ashbery. Los Angeles: University of California Press, 1995. Page 197.

373. O'Hara, Frank. "BIOTHERM (FOR BILL BERKSON)." Line 71. *The Collected Poems of Frank O'Hara*. Edited by Donald Allen. Introduction by John Ashbery. Los Angeles: University of California Press, 1995. Page 438.

374. O'Hara, Frank. "[STATEMENT FOR *THE NEW AMERICAN POETRY*]." Line 5. *The Collected Poems of Frank O'Hara*. Edited by Donald Allen. Introduction by John Ashbery. Los Angeles: University of California Press, 1995. Page 500.

www.ingramcontent.com/pod-product-compliance
Lightning Source LLC
LaVergne TN
LVHW051102080426
835508LV00019B/2013